Decorating With
Paint & Wallcovering

COWLES
Creative Publishing

A Division of Cowles Enthusiast Media, Inc.

Contents

Copyright © 1988
Cowles Creative Publishing, Inc.
Formerly Cy DeCosse Incorporated
5900 Green Oak Drive
Minnetonka, Minnesota 55343
1-800-328-3895
All rights reserved
Printed in U.S.A.

Also available from the publisher:
 Everyday Home Repairs, Carpentry: Tools •
 Shelves • Walls • Doors, Kitchen Remodeling,
 Building Decks, Home Plumbing Projects
 & Repairs, Basic Wiring & Electrical Repairs,
 Workshop Tips & Techniques, Advanced
 Home Wiring, Carpentry: Remodeling,
 Landscape Design & Construction, Bathroom
 Remodeling, Built-in Projects for the Home,
 Kitchen & Bathroom Ideas, Refinishing &
 Finishing Wood, Exterior Home Repairs &
 Improvements, Home Masonry Repairs &
 Projects, Building Porches & Patios, Deck
 & Landscape Ideas

Library of Congress
Cataloging-in-Publication Data
Decorating With Paint & Wallcovering

(Black & Decker home improvement library)
Includes index. 1. House painting. 2. Paper-
hanging. 3. Interior decorations - Amateurs'
manuals.
I. Cy DeCosse Incorporated. II. Title:
Decorating with paint and wallcovering.
III. Series.
TH323 D43 1988 747'.3 dc19 88-9558 CIP
ISBN 0-86573-702-9 (hardcover).
ISBN 0-86573-703-7 (softcover).

COWLES
Creative Publishing
A Division of Cowles Enthusiast Media, Inc.

President/COO: Nino Tarantino
Executive V.P./Editor-in-Chief:
 William B. Jones

DECORATING WITH PAINT &
WALLCOVERING
Created by: The editors of Cowles
Creative Publishing, in cooperation with
Black & Decker. ● BLACK&DECKER is a
trademark of the Black & Decker
Corporation and is used under license.

Project Director: Gary D. Branson
Project Manager: Barbara Lund
Editor: Bryan Trandem
Art Director & Room Set Designer:
 Barbara Falk
Senior Art Director: Tim J. Himsel
Project Consultants: Bernie Maehren,
 Lynette Reber
Production Manager: Jim Bindas
Assistant Production Managers:
 Julie Churchill, Jacquie Marx
Production Staff: Janice Cauley, Sheila
 DiPaola, Joe Fahey, Carol Kevan, Yelena
 Konrardy, Cindy Natvig, Dave Schelitzche,
 Linda Schloegel, Jennie Smith, Greg
 Wallace, Nik Wogstad

Studio Manager: Cathleen Shannon
Photographers: Rex Irmen, Tony Kubat,
 John Lauenstein, Bill Lindner, Mark
 Macemon, Mette Nielsen
Contributing Photographers: Rudy Calin,
 Dan Halsey
Contributing Copywriter: Susan Christy
Design Consultants: Jennifer Burger,
 Kate Halverson
Wallcovering Consultants: Cathy Colvin,
 Jerry Sartor
Painting Consultant: Jack Andrashko
Set Builders: Paul Currie, Phil Hinz
Contributing Individuals and Agencies:
 National Decorating Products Association,
 Pat Stewart, University of Minnesota
 Entomology Department

Contributing Manufacturers: American Brush
 Company, Inc.; Cooper Industries
 (including registered trademarks:
 Crescent, Lufkin, Nicholson, Plumb,
 Turner, Weller, Wire-Wrap, Wiss, Xcelite);
 Muralo/Elder Jenks; The Stanley Works

COWLES
Enthusiast Media
President/COO: Philip L. Penny

Printed on American paper by:
 R. R. Donnelley & Sons Co.
99 98 97 96 / 5 4 3 2 1

Introduction

At the Black & Decker Home Improvement Library, our goal is to provide our readers with home repair information they can use. From remodeling industry data, we know that 94% of homeowners do at least some of their own interior decorating. *Decorating With Paint & Wallcovering* provides a needed addition to any homeowner's library.

We invited professional decorators and designers to put together the most useful decorating information, ideas and tips. We divided that information into four easy-to-use parts.

The first section, "Room Design," starts with an introduction to color that will help you make your own choices. We decorated and photographed the same room 34 times to help you visualize what a difference color, texture and pattern can make in a room. You can duplicate any decorating style in this section for the price of a gallon of paint or a few rolls of wallcovering.

When you have made your decisions on color and style, move on to the second section, "Preparation." Here you will find information that includes the latest methods and materials for repairing wallboard and

plaster, and preparing walls and woodwork for refinishing. The section concludes with advice on when and how to use primers and sealers to ensure the best results when painting.

The third section, "Painting," shows you how to estimate the amount of paint you need to buy, how to choose the right kind of paint, and how to choose, use and store the proper painting tools for best results. This section also includes tips on painting safety, how to clean up with minimum effort when the job is finished and how to safely dispose of paint materials.

"Wallcovering," our final section, is a seminar on wallcovering installation techniques. In addition to general advice on wallcovering procedures, we show you how to hang wallcovering on ceilings, how to get around obstacles like radiators and pipes, and how to wallcover recessed windows and round archways.

This book has more than 380 color photos to clearly illustrate the step-by-step procedures. This book will provide you with a decorating reference that you will use year after year.

Room Design

28 TH 19 FROSTY MORNING (W)

28 TH 20 BRISK BLUE (W)

28 TH 21 BITTERCOLD (W)

The Dimensions of Color

Light

Value

Dark

Neutral

Subdued

Bright

Hue

Warm ← ——— Color temperature ——— → Cool

Color Basics

A new color scheme can dramatically change a room or your entire home. Even without changing expensive furniture or carpeting, a fresh infusion of color can transform the most ordinary room into an inviting living space.

Since color is a very personal choice, start your decorating scheme with colors you enjoy, such as those in your clothing, furnishings or artwork. Look for ideas in magazines. Browse decorating centers for paint colors, wallcoverings and fabric. Look at paint and wallcovering samples in your own home, using the 24-hour test (page 31). Color can look significantly different, depending on the lighting conditions and the surroundings.

Colors can be light or dark, warm or cool, bright or subdued. A color scheme sets the mood for the room, so choose colors that create the feeling you desire.

Glossary of Color Terms

Accent Color: A contrasting hue used to add visual interest in a color scheme

Color Scheme: A group of colors used together to create a mood or effect

Complementary Colors: Two colors directly opposite one another on the color wheel

Complementary Color Scheme: The use of complementary colors in a decorating plan

Contrasting Colors: Colors that have at least three other colors between them on the color wheel

Cool Colors: Blues, greens, purples

Desaturated Colors: Subdued hues; colors made less brilliant by the addition of white, black or complementary color

Hue: A color

Neutral Colors: Subtle variations of whites, grays, beiges

Primary Colors: Red, yellow and blue

Related Colors: Two colors next to one another on the color wheel

Related Color Scheme: The use of related colors in a decorating plan

Saturated Colors: Bright hues; intense colors undiluted by black, white or complementary color

Secondary Colors: Orange, green and purple; colors formed by mixing two primary colors

Shade: A darker hue variation, created by adding black or gray

Single-color Scheme: The use of varying shades of a single hue in a decorating plan

Tint: A lighter hue variation, created by adding white

Value: The scale of lightness or darkness of a color

Warm Colors: Reds, oranges, yellows and browns

The color wheel shows how colors are related. Red, yellow and blue are primary colors. Orange, green and purple are secondary colors made by combining two primary colors. All colors are made from some combination of white, black and primary colors.

Related colors are those next to one another on the color wheel. Designers often build color schemes around two or three related colors.

Complementary colors are located opposite each other on the color wheel. Blue, for example, is the complement of orange. Complementary colors enhance each other in decorating schemes.

Neutral colors are shades of white, gray or beige. Most neutrals are tinted slightly with a warm or cool color. Neutral-colored walls provide a backdrop that does not compete with furnishings and accessories.

Light Colors

Light colors create bright, spacious rooms. To the eye, light colors seem to recede, making rooms appear larger and ceilings higher. Since light colors reflect the most light, they can brighten a north-facing room, a closet or dark hallway.

Whites and other light colors are good choices for a nursery or child's bedroom. In any room, white walls form a neutral background that does not compete with furnishings.

Wall roughness and paint sheen can affect the lightness of any color. Smooth surfaces and gloss paints reflect maximum light to make a color seem lighter. Rough-textured walls and flat-sheen paints hold more shadow and minimize the lightness of a color.

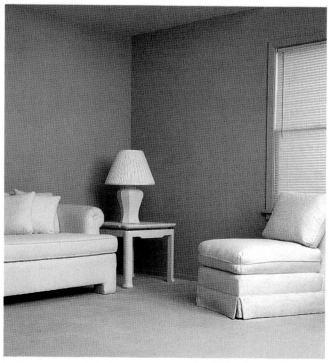

Light colors reflect light, which makes rooms appear larger and more open. In these rooms, the light furnishings blend with the walls to increase the open feeling. Use light wall colors in small rooms or in rooms with little natural light. Light colors help brighten a nursery or child's bedroom.

Dark Colors

Use dark colors to create an intimate room. Because dark colors absorb light, walls appear closer to make the room seem smaller. Dark colors are most often used in libraries, studies and other quiet areas.

Darker colors can be used to disguise problem areas such as uneven walls, or to make a high ceiling seem lower. In heavy-use areas, dark colors can help hide wear. Rough surfaces and flat paint finishes make colors seem darker because they absorb more light.

Dark walls tend to dominate, so you may choose to use lighter-colored accents to add balance to a room.

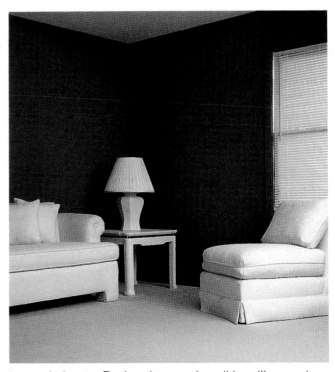

Dark colors absorb light to make a room seem quieter and more intimate. Dark colors work well in a library, den or study. Dark-colored walls in these rooms emphasize the light furnishings. Darker furnishings would blend into this type of room, creating a heavier atmosphere.

Warm Colors

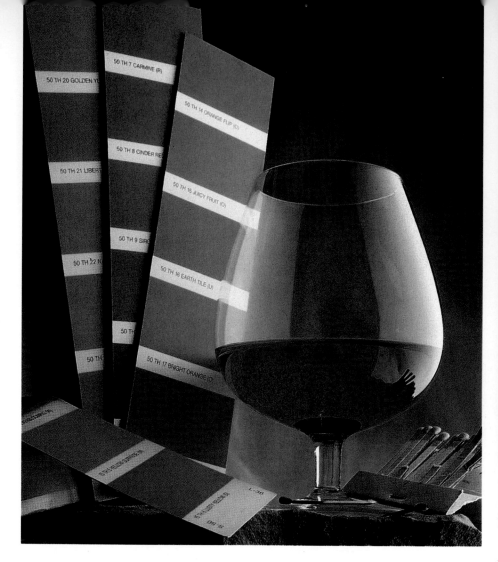

Reds, yellows, browns, oranges and peaches are warm colors. Intense warm colors create exciting spaces, while subdued warm colors form pleasant rooms for social gatherings. Warm colors are often used in eating areas, like breakfast or dining rooms.

Warm colors also help make north rooms more inviting. Research has shown that people actually feel warmer in a room painted with yellows, reds or oranges than they do in a white or blue room. In colder climates, warm colors are a popular choice.

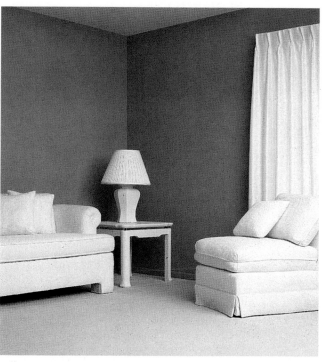

Warm colors range from intense yellows, reds and oranges to more subtle salmons and browns. Warm colors are common choices for morning rooms, or for active nighttime spaces. In colder climates, warm colors can make rooms seem cozy and more inviting.

Cool Colors

Blues, greens, lavenders and grays are cool colors. Intense cool colors are fresh and dramatic, while subdued cool grays are tranquil. Cool colors make rooms feel less confining. They are often used in bathrooms and other small rooms.

Use cool colors in west-facing kitchens, porches and other areas where afternoon heat is a problem. In very warm climates, using whites and cool colors exclusively can make an entire house seem more comfortable.

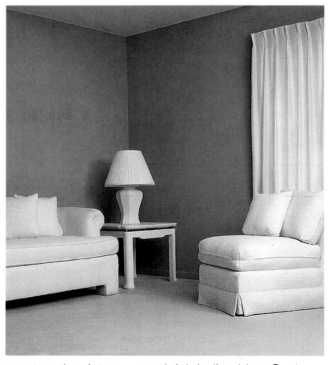

Cool colors range from bright violet, royal blue and jade green to pale mint green and rich indigo blue. Cool colors are frequently used in bedrooms and in formal living and dining areas. Bathrooms, dressing rooms and other small spaces feel less confining when decorated in cool colors.

Bright Colors

Bright colors are highly saturated with pigment. They are not diluted by white or darkened by black. Bright colors work well in active spaces like recreation rooms, sun porches and children's rooms.

Because bright colors draw attention, they are often used as accents in rooms with neutral or subdued color schemes.

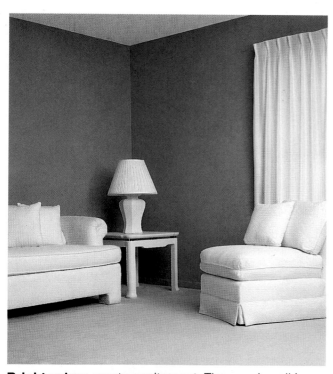

Bright colors create excitement. They work well in active, informal spaces. Bright colors also work well in rooms with little natural light, such as basement recreation rooms.

14

Subdued Colors

Subdued colors are less saturated with pigment than bright colors. They are blended to include mixtures of white, black or gray. Subdued colors are relaxing and restful, and are frequently used in studies and bedrooms. Subdued colors form a soft background in bathrooms and dressing rooms.

You can increase visual interest in a subdued room by adding a few brightly colored accents.

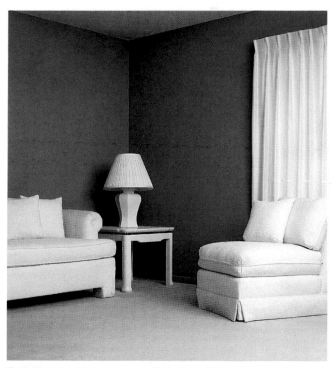

Subdued colors are restful. Use them to create a tranquil mood in bedrooms and other quiet retreats.

Creating Moods with Color

Each color or combination of colors inspires a different feeling or mood. The color should appeal to the people who use the room. The combinations you may choose are limitless.

For an entryway or foyer, consider a bold color combination that makes a strong introduction to your home. For a guest bedroom, you might choose classic dark colors to create an elegant, formal feeling. In a teenager's bedroom, a surprising mixture of bright colors can be appropriate. In a master bedroom, you might be more comfortable with a restful combination of subdued colors.

In a library or study that is used by the whole family, you may use soft, related colors that create a tranquil mood. Natural tones like browns and beiges are a good choice for libraries and family rooms.

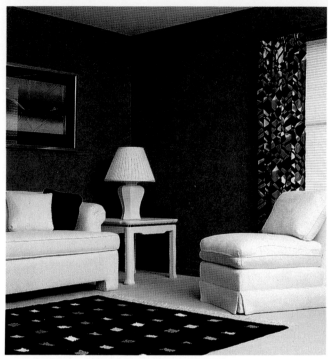

Bold color scheme in this room is created by the high contrast between whites and blacks, and between the complementary red and green. Hard-edged geometric patterns and dark walls contribute to the striking design.

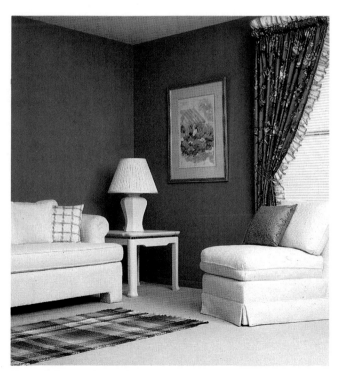

Surprising color scheme uses several bright colors and fabrics. The unusual combination of fabric patterns adds to the dramatic effect.

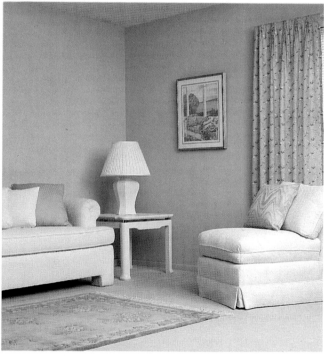

Tranquil room is created by using cool related colors that have low contrast. The floral patterns repeated in the draperies, artwork and rug help unify the room.

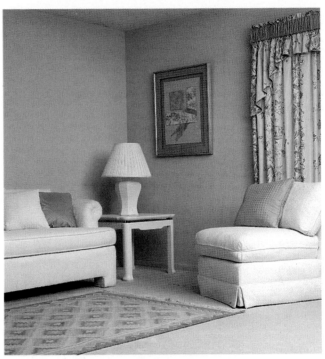

Cheerful and airy mood is created by light colors that make the room seem larger. To maintain the open feeling, low-contrast pastel colors were chosen for the furnishings. The minimal window treatment opens the room to maximum sunlight.

Subtle, comfortable decorating scheme uses subdued complementary colors. The carefully placed pastel blues provide a cool contrast to the warm peach-colored walls.

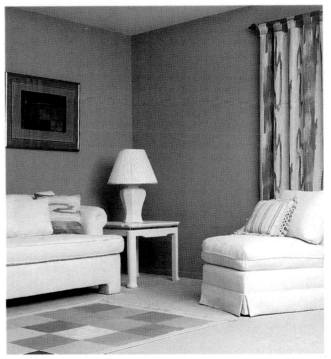

Formal decorating scheme uses classically detailed patterns, rich fabrics and dark accent colors that draw attention. A darker wall would give this room a more intimate feeling.

Natural color scheme is created by using warm earth tones with simple patterns and textures. The sky blues in this room provide a cool accent to the natural warmth of the brown tones.

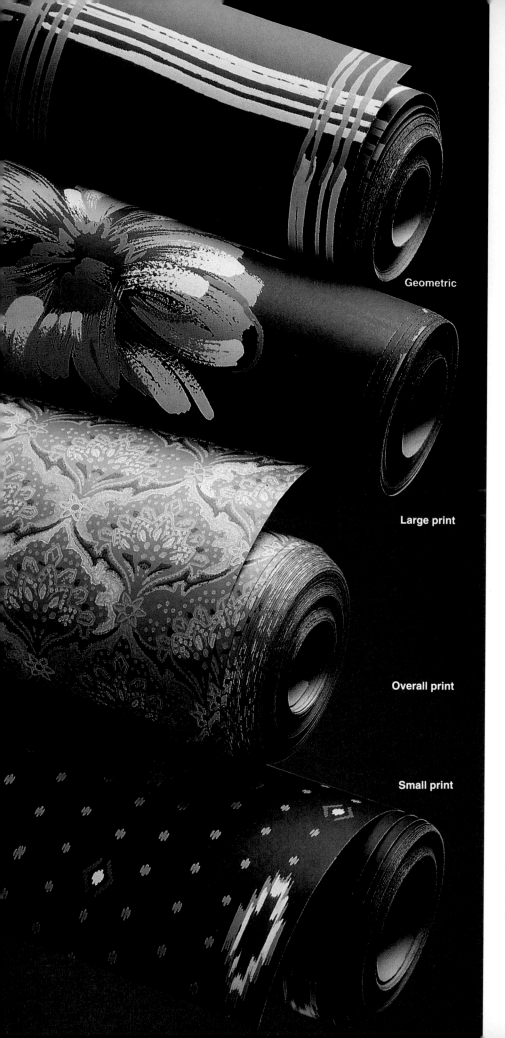

Geometric

Large print

Overall print

Small print

Pattern Basics

Wallcoverings increase visual interest by adding pattern, texture and accent color to a room. They are a dramatic way to quickly define a room style. For example, a bold abstract print immediately establishes a contemporary style, while a small floral design will suggest a more traditional or country theme.

Many vinyl wallcoverings are washable and are increasingly popular choices for kitchens, baths and high-traffic areas.

Your decorating center offers hundreds of different wallcovering designs that fall into four basic styles (shown at left): geometrics, large prints, overall prints and small prints. Many centers have decorating consultants who will help you with style and pattern selections at no charge.

Basic Wallcovering Patterns

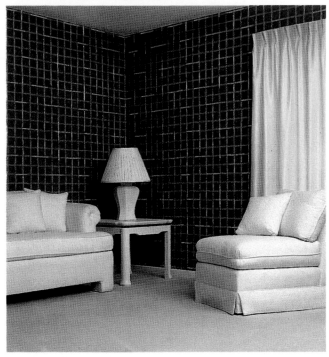

Geometric patterns include plaids, stripes and grids. Large geometric patterns can be bold and exciting, while small patterns can be very subtle. Patterns with strong vertical lines make a ceiling seem higher.

Large prints add the most visual interest to a room. They can also make a room seem smaller and more intimate.

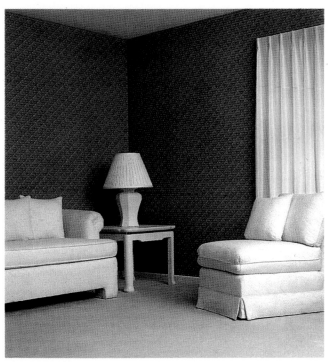

Overall prints form tight patterns. The eye blends the design together, minimizing pattern and emphasizing color. Overall prints can be used in any room.

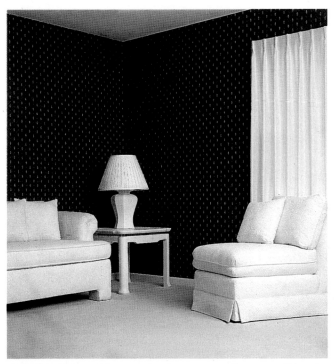

Small prints add a touch of pattern to the overall background color, forming a subtle backdrop. They are often used in kitchens, bathrooms and other small spaces.

Special Effects

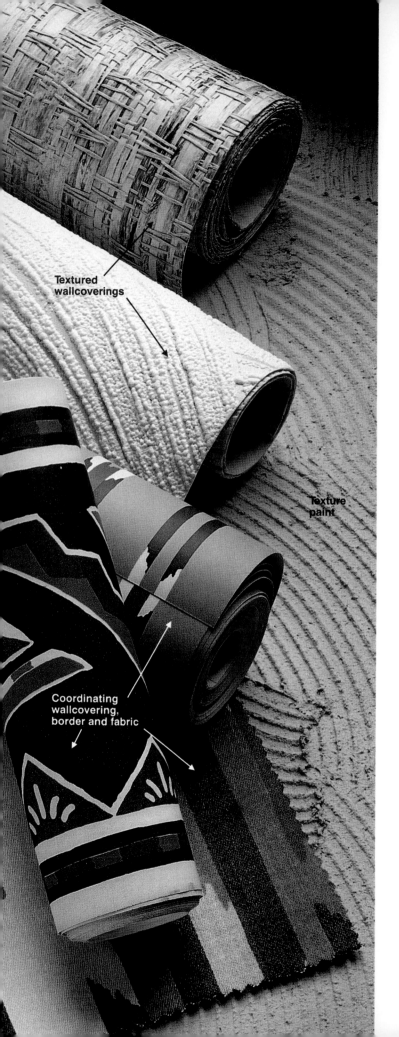

Textured
wallcoverings

Texture
paint

Coordinating
wallcovering,
border and fabric

Wallcoverings with coordinated fabrics, borders and textured surfaces expand your decorating options. Linen, grasscloth or textile wallcoverings will soften the appearance of a room. Embossed or expanded vinyl wallcoverings give walls three-dimensional texture. Texture paint is an inexpensive way to add interest or cover up an uneven surface.

Many manufacturers produce fabrics and borders that coordinate with wallcoverings. Wallcovering books contain samples of each, and may have photos showing how the elements can be combined. These photos offer a good source of ideas for wall treatments.

Sample books group coordinated wallcoverings, borders and fabrics. Sample books may have photos that show you how the elements can be combined.

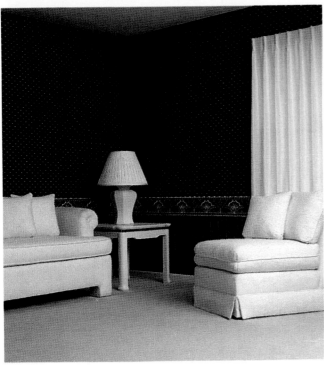

Borders add interest. They can be used to blend co-ordinated wallcoverings, to frame windows, doors and ceilings, or as a chair rail on painted walls.

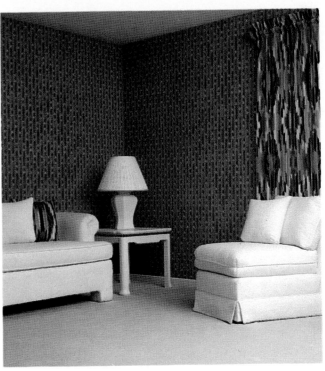

Coordinating fabrics and wallcoverings are available from manufacturers. Fabrics may match the wallcoverings or be complementary. The coordinates may also include matching or complementary borders.

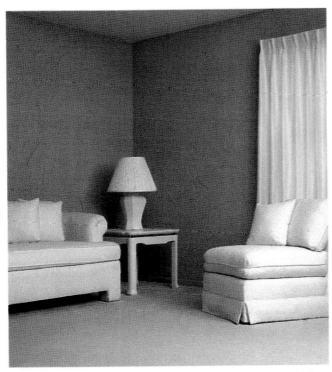

Texture paint creates shadows and slight color differences for a more interesting wall surface. Working the wet paint with different tools produces a variety of texture effects (pages 84-85).

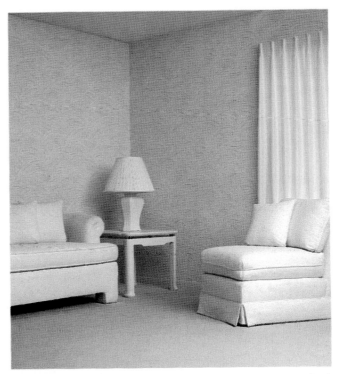

Textured wallcoverings, like embossed or expanded vinyls, imitate the effect of plaster or texture paint on walls and ceilings. Textured wallcoverings have the added benefit of being easy to remove.

Creating Your Own Room Design

A successful decorating plan creatively blends the old with the new. Start by collecting samples from the furniture, carpeting or other elements you want to retain in the room.

Take a small sample of carpeting from an inconspicuous area, like a closet. Clip fabric swatches from hems and folds of upholstery and drapes. If possible, take samples of woodwork and tiles.

Next, visit decorating centers to collect samples of paint colors and wallcoverings. Clip out interesting ideas from magazines. As you assemble samples, spread them out in the room you intend to decorate. Try to imagine how new colors and patterns might look next to the existing furnishings. The best decorating scheme is one that pleases you and your family, so trust your own judgment when choosing colors and patterns.

Snip samples from inside drapery hems, and take samples of carpet threads from closet corners. Cut samples of upholstery fabrics from the undersides of furniture. Collect samples of flooring tiles and woodwork, if possible.

Clip ideas from decorating magazines, and collect paint, wallcovering and fabric samples during visits to home decorating centers.

Tape or staple samples to index cards. Use the cards to jot down measurements or to make small sketches and notes. Place samples in clear plastic bags so that you can see the contents easily. You will find this particularly useful if you are working on more than one room. Take your samples along to the decorating center as you begin making selections.

Building a Basic Color Scheme

Most room designs use one of three basic color schemes. A **single-color scheme** uses one color in varying shades, like light and dark blues. A **related color scheme** features colors that are next to each other on the color wheel. A room decorated in blues and lavenders is an example of a related color scheme. A **complementary color scheme** uses colors that are opposite each other on the color wheel, like peach and blue.

When redecorating a room, you can create a wide variety of color schemes even if the carpeting and furnishings remain the same.

Single-color Scheme

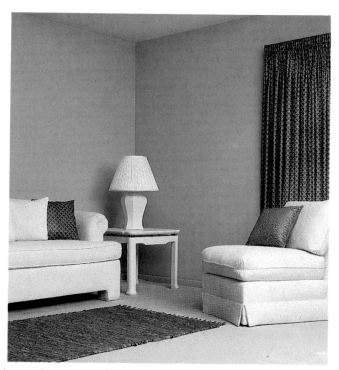

Use varying shades of the same color. A single-color scheme is easy to develop, and it lends a restful feeling to a room. You can tie two rooms together by using the same single-color scheme in both spaces. The choice of darker blues in this room allows the lighter furnishings to stand out.

Related Color Scheme

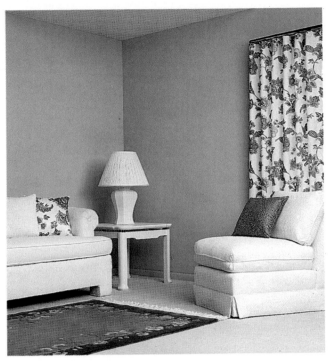

Use colors that are close together on the color wheel. A related color scheme creates a unified, quiet room. Related light colors are relaxing, while related dark colors are elegant and formal.

Complementary Color Scheme

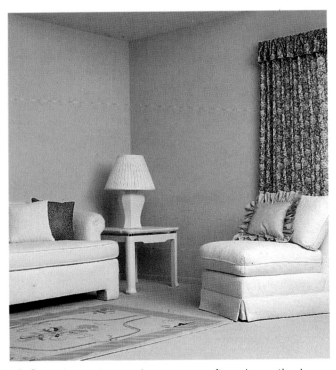

Use colors found opposite each other on the color wheel. Complementary schemes are often dramatic. In this room, the warm peach is enhanced and balanced by cool blue accents. The lighter pastel walls allow the light-colored furnishings to blend into the room.

Decorating with Coordinates

Coordinated collections of fabrics, wallcoverings and borders give you great flexibility in designing a room. By using the same fabric in draperies, pillows and furniture slipcovers, you can unify a room.

To highlight furnishings, choose a wallcovering or paint that contrasts with the furniture and the draperies. To call less attention to furnishings, choose wallcovering and paint colors that blend with them.

A well-designed room may use only one pattern or many different patterns that are related by color or style.

Low-contrast Scheme

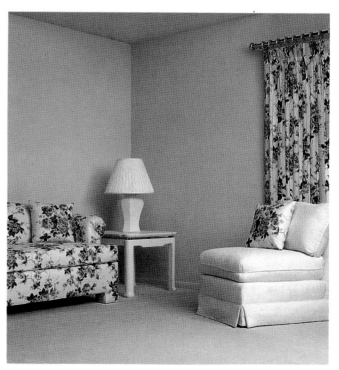

A single pattern in the fabric helps unify the draperies and furniture. The wall color was chosen to match the light background color in the fabric. This makes the room seem larger by helping the furniture blend into walls. Repeating the same pattern will help to unify adjoining rooms.

High-contrast Scheme

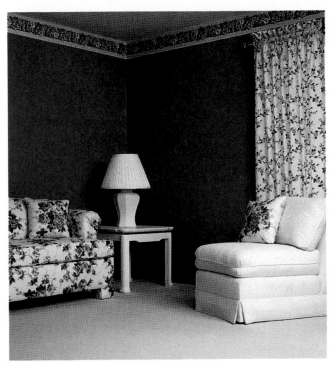

The dark green in the fabric is used as the background wall color to form a strong contrast with the light carpeting and upholstery fabrics. The detailed pattern in the wallcovering border contrasts with the solid colors surrounding it.

Multi-pattern Scheme

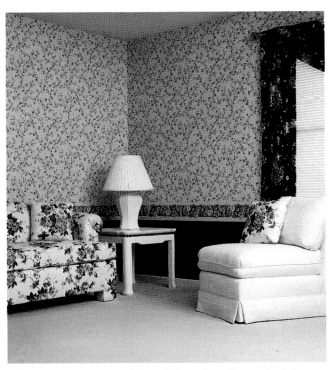

Several different patterns can be combined successfully in the same room. The different patterns in this room are unified by related floral designs and repeated colors. The wallcovering border helps blend the room elements together.

Selecting Paint & Wallcovering

When you begin shopping for a new paint color or wallcovering, bring fabric swatches and other samples of your home furnishings to the decorating center.

Many decorating centers have professional design consultants who help customers at no charge. The paint selection display in a home decorating center can hold more than a thousand different colors, and wallcovering departments may have several hundred sample books. By comparing the samples from your home with the store's paint swatches and wallcovering samples, you can narrow your selections quickly.

Always bring several paint or wallcovering samples back to your home for a day or two before making a final selection. Look at the samples in the room you are decorating to see how the colors and patterns interact with the existing furnishings. Remember that colors change under different lighting conditions, so look at your samples in bright daylight, on a cloudy day and under artificial light.

Tips for Selecting Paint & Wallcovering

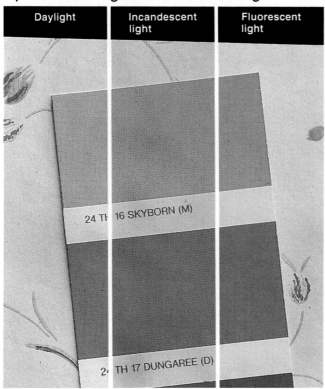

Daylight	Incandescent light	Fluorescent light

24 TH 16 SKYBORN (M)

24 TH 17 DUNGAREE (D)

In the store, check paint chips and wallcovering samples in daylight as well as under artificial lighting. Store lighting can differ from home lighting.

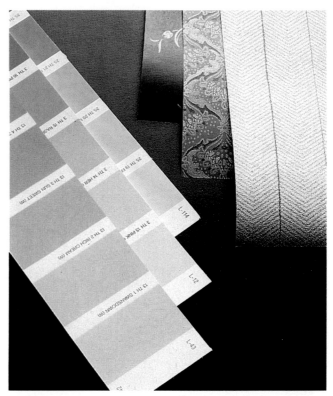

Take home no more than 3 different color and wall-covering samples. Fewer alternatives make the final decision easier.

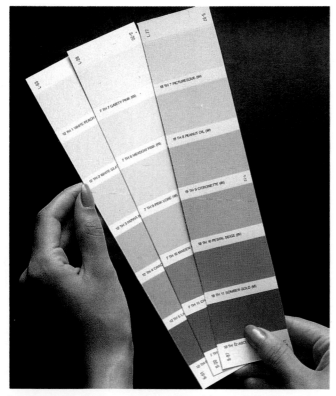

Look at the dark end of a paint chip card to determine the tint base of an off-white paint. Almost all off-whites have a hint of color.

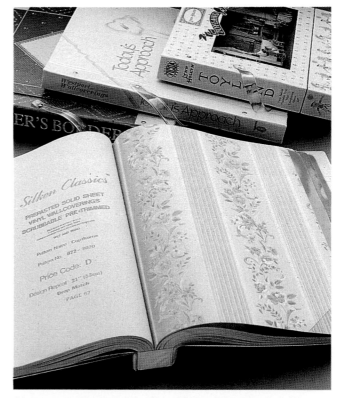

Choose wallcovering books by flipping quickly through them. A quick glance saves time and can tell you which books you will want to study more carefully.

(continued next page)

Tape 4 paint chips together. Larger color samples are easier to judge. Cut off white borders, which can be distracting.

Judge samples of paint and wallcovering in the room where they will be used. Stand color samples upright to duplicate the way light strikes a wall surface. Tape wallcovering samples against the walls where they will be hung.

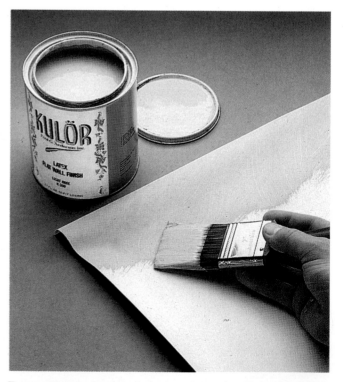

Before making final decision, cut a large sample of wallcovering to use in the 24-hour test (page opposite). Decorating centers will usually give large samples, or may let you borrow sample books.

Buy a quart of your chosen paint color. Paint a large sample card to hang on the wall. Follow the 24-hour test (page opposite) before buying the full amounts of paint and wallcovering needed.

The 24-Hour Test

Lighting affects color. To judge how paint or wall-covering will really look before making your final decision, hang a large sample on the wall and check it from time to time over the course of a 24-hour day. Notice how the color changes under varying lighting situations. If a room is most often used at a particular time of day, look at the color carefully at this time. Paint and wallcovering colors will look different in your home than they do in the decorating center. Furniture, woodwork and floors reflect their own colors onto the walls, changing their appearance.

Incandescent indoor lighting generally has a yellow cast, although the choice of light bulb and shade can change its tint.

Natural daylight has a blue cast at midday, but has a warm orange tint at sunrise and sunset.

Preparation

Ladders & Scaffolds

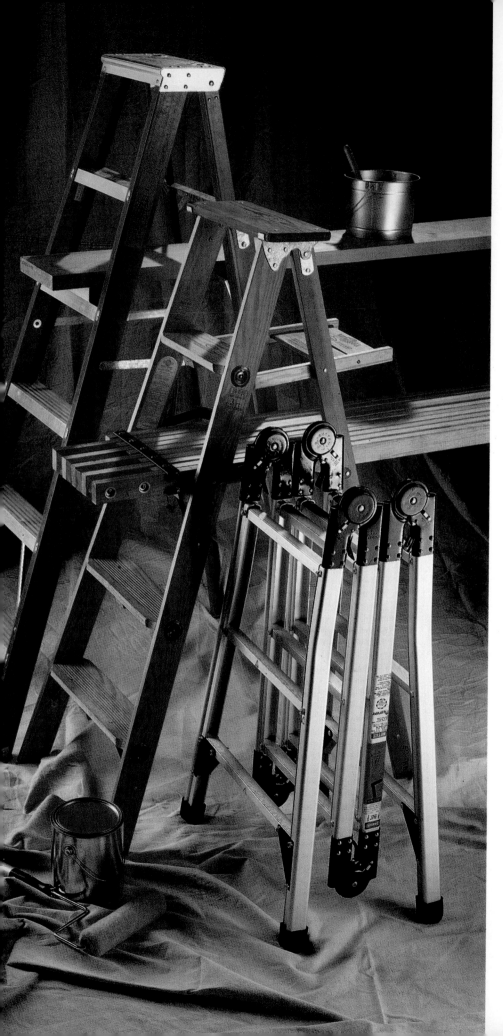

Two quality stepladders and an extension plank are all you need to paint most interior surfaces. For painting high areas, build a simple scaffold by running the plank through the steps of two stepladders. It is easy to lose your balance or step off the plank, so choose tall ladders for safety. The upper part of the ladders can help you balance, and will keep you from stepping off the ends of the plank. Buy a strong, straight 2 × 10-inch plank no more than 12 feet long, or rent a plank from a material dealer or rental outlet.

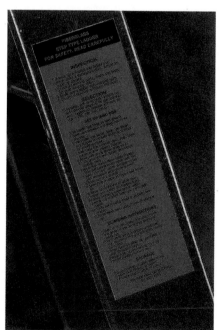

Manufacturer's sticker gives weight ratings and instructions for correct use of the ladder. Read it carefully when shopping for a ladder. Remember that you may exceed its recommended weight limits when you carry tools or materials up a ladder.

How to Use a Scaffold

For ceilings and high spots on walls, make a simple scaffold by running an extension plank through the steps of 2 stepladders. Plank should be no more than 12 feet long. Ladders should face away from one another, so that steps are to inside. Make sure the ladder braces are down and locked, and watch your footing.

How to Use a Scaffold on Stairways

For stairs run an extension plank through the step of a ladder, and place the other end on a stairway step. Make sure the ladder is steady, and check to see that the plank is level. Keep the plank close to the wall, if possible, and never overreach.

Rent extension planks from a paint dealer or from a rental center.

Choose straight planks without large knots or splinters. Choose 2 × 10" boards that have some spring in them: stiff, brittle wooden planks can break unexpectedly.

Push braces completely down and make certain they are locked. Legs of the ladder should be level and steady against the ground.

Do not stand on top step, top brace or on the utility shelf of a stepladder.

Center your weight on the ladder. Move the ladder often: don't overreach.

Keep steps tight by periodically checking them and tightening the braces when they need it.

Keep ladder in front of you when working. Lean your body against the ladder for balance.

Adjustable ladder adapts to many different work needs. It can be used as a straight ladder, a stepladder or as a base for scaffold planks.

Work light

Drop cloth

Sprayer

Bucket & natural sponge

Rubber gloves

Palm sander

Wet sander

Wallboard knives

Hand vacuum

Heat gun

Screw gun

Perforation tool

Paint brush

Tools & Materials for Preparation

You can reduce or eliminate most cleanup chores by buying the right prep tools. For example, buy plastic or paper throwaway pails for mixing patching plaster, taping compound or spackle. When the patcher hardens in the container, just throw it away: you'll avoid the job of washing out the pail and also avoid plugging plumbing drains with plaster.

Use a sponge or wallboard wet sander to smooth plaster or wallboard compound while it is still soft,

rather than waiting until it dries and becomes hard to sand.

Buy a variety of patching tools. You will need narrow putty knives for reaching into small spaces, and a wider knife or trowel that just spans the repair area when patching holes in walls or ceilings. A patching tool that overlaps both edges of the hole will let you patch with one pass of the tool, reducing trowel marks and eliminating sanding.

Removal agents help prepare surfaces for paint and wallcovering, and speed cleanup. Clockwise from top left: wallpaper dough, cleanup solution, wallcovering remover, trisodium phosphate (TSP).

Preparation liquids, clockwise from top left: paint remover, liquid deglosser for dulling glossy surfaces prior to painting, latex bonding agent for plaster repairs.

Patching and masking products, clockwise from top left: patching plaster, masking tape, premixed wallboard compound, fiberglass wallboard tape, wood patch, peel-and-stick metal patch, pregummed masking paper.

Primer & sealers provide a good base coat that bonds with paint or varnish finish. From left: sanding sealer, PVA primer, shellac, alkyd wallboard primer.

Preparing the Room

How to Prepare a Room

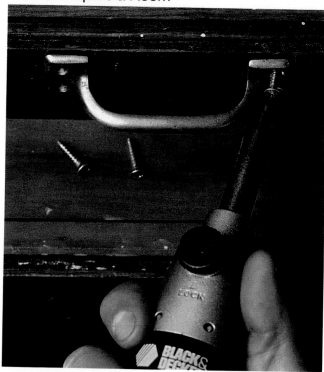

Before painting, your first step is to protect everything that could be splattered by paint. Remove all window and door hardware, light fixtures, and the coverplates on outlets and wall switches. Drape furniture and cover the floors. Remove heating and air conditioning duct covers. Mask off wood moldings with self-adhesive paper or masking tape.

Tip: When removing hardware, mark the pieces with masking tape for identification so that they can be replaced easily.

1 Remove all hardware, such as window handles and cabinet catches, from surfaces to be painted. If you will be installing new hardware, buy it now and drill new screw holes if needed.

2 Remove all nails, screws and picture hangers from surfaces to be painted. To prevent damage to the plaster or wallboard, use a block of wood under the head of the hammer.

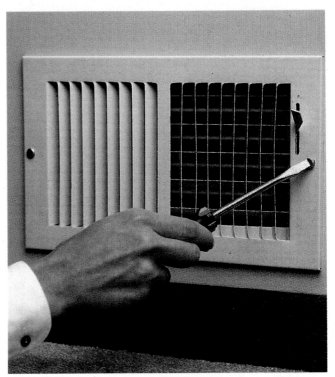

3 Remove covers from heating and air-conditioning ducts to protect them from splatters. Remove thermostats, or use masking tape to protect them against paint drips.

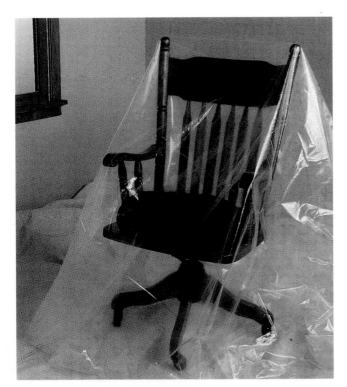

4 Move furniture to center of room and cover with sheets of plastic. In a large room, leave an alley through center of room for access if painting the ceiling. Cover floors with 9-ounce canvas drop cloths. Canvas absorbs paint spills.

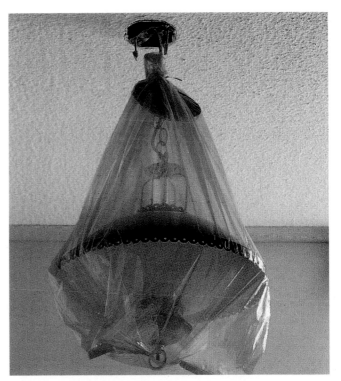

5 Turn off electricity. Remove coverplates from outlets and switches. Return cover screws to screw holes. Drop light fixtures away from electrical boxes, or remove the fixtures. Cover hanging fixtures with plastic bags.

Removing Wallcovering

Newer vinyl wallcoverings can often be peeled off by hand. Some will leave a paper and adhesive residue that is easily removed with water. With non-peelable wallcoverings, pierce the surface with a perforation tool, then apply remover solution to dissolve the adhesive.

Wallcovering remover fluids contain wetting agents that penetrate the paper and help soften the adhesive. Use a remover solution to wash away old adhesive after wallcovering is removed.

If the old wallcovering was hung over unsealed wallboard, it may be impossible to remove it without destroying the wallboard. You may be able to paint or hang new wallcovering directly over the old wallcovering, but the surface should be smooth and primed. Before painting over wallcovering, prime with alkyd wallboard primer.

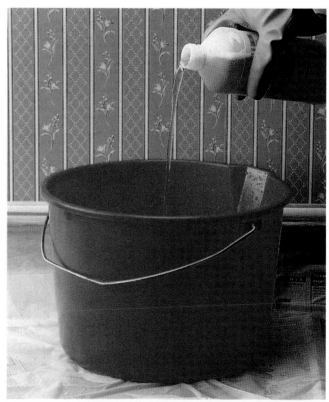

1 Find a loose edge and try to strip wallcovering. Vinyls often peel away easily.

2 If wallcovering does not strip by hand, cover floor with layers of newspaper. Add wallcovering remover fluid to bucket of water, as directed by manufacturer.

3 Pierce the surface of wallcovering with perforation tool. This allows the remover solution to enter and soften the adhesive.

4 Use a sprayer, paint roller or sponge to apply remover solution. Let moisture soak into covering, according to manufacturer's directions.

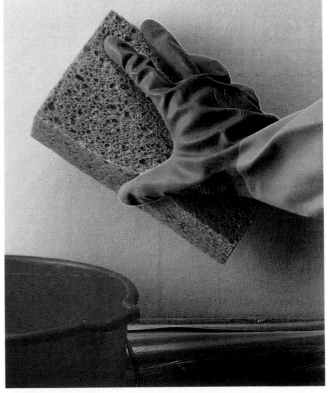

5 Peel away loosened wallcovering with a 6-inch broadknife. Be careful not to damage the plaster or wallboard. Remove all backing paper.

6 Rinse adhesive residue from wall with remover solution. Rinse with clear water and let walls dry completely.

Preparing & Repairing Walls & Ceilings

Thoroughly washing, rinsing and sanding your walls before priming will guarantee a long-lasting finish. For a professional appearance, carefully check your walls for damage and repair the wallboard or plaster as needed. Pregummed fiberglass repair tapes and premixed patching compounds reduce drying time and let you patch and paint a wall the same day.

Wash and sand before repainting. Use TSP (trisodium phosphate) solution and a sponge to cut grease and to remove dirt. Wear rubber gloves, and wash walls from the bottom up with a damp sponge to avoid streaks. Rinse thoroughly with clean water. After drying, sand surfaces lightly.

How to Remove Stains

1 Apply stain remover to a clean, dry cloth, and rub lightly to remove the stain.

2 Seal all stain areas with white pigmented shellac. Pigmented shellac prevents stains from bleeding through the new paint.

Water or rust stains may indicate water damage. Check for leaking pipes and soft plaster, make needed repairs, then seal area with stain-killing sealer.

How to Remove Mildew

1 Test stains by washing with water and detergent. Mildew stains will not wash out.

2 Wearing rubber gloves and eye protection, wash the walls with bleach, which kills mildew spores.

3 After bleach treatment, wash mildew away with TSP solution, and rinse with clear water.

How to Patch Peeling Paint

1 Scrape away loose paint with a putty knife or paint scraper.

2 Apply spackle to the edges of chipped paint with a putty knife or flexible wallboard knife.

3 Sand the patch area with 150-grit production sandpaper. Patch area should feel smooth to the touch.

How to Fill Nail Holes

1 Apply lightweight spackle to the hole with a putty knife or your fingertip. This keeps repair area small so it is easy to hide with paint. Let spackle dry.

2 Sand the repair area lightly with 150-grit production sandpaper. Production paper has an open surface that does not clog. Wipe dust away with a damp sponge, then prime the spot with PVA primer.

How to Fill Shallow Dents & Holes

1 Scrape or sand away any loose plaster, peeled paint or wallboard face paper to ensure a solid base for patching.

2 Fill hole with lightweight spackle. Apply spackle with smallest wallboard knife that will span the entire hole. Let spackle dry.

3 Sand lightly with 150-grit production sandpaper.

How to Fix Popped Wallboard Nails

1 Drive wallboard screw 2" away from popped nail. Be sure the screw hits the stud or joist and pulls the wallboard tight against the framing.

2 Scrape away loose paint or wallboard compound. Drive the popped nail back into the framing so the head is sunk 1/32" below the surface of the wallboard. Do not set the nail with a punch.

3 Use wallboard knife to apply 3 coats of premixed wallboard compound to nail and screw holes. Allow drying time after each coat. Compound will shrink. Sand and spot-prime the patch area.

How to Repair Cracks in Plaster

1 Scrape away any texture or loose plaster around the crack. Reinforce crack with pregummed fiberglass wallboard tape.

2 Use taping knife or trowel to apply spackle or wallboard compound over tape so that tape is just concealed: if compound is too thick, it will recrack.

3 Apply a second thin coat if necessary to conceal the tape edges. Sand lightly and prime the repair area. Retexture the surface (pages 84-85).

How to Patch Small Holes in Wallboard

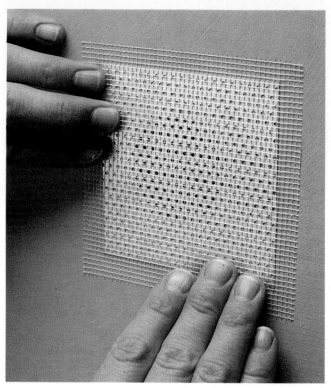

1 Inspect the damaged area. If there are no cracks around the edge of the hole, just fill the hole with spackle, let dry and sand it smooth.

2 If edges are cracked, cover hole with peel-and-stick repair patch. The patch has a metal mesh center for strength, and can be cut or shaped as needed. Patches are available in several sizes.

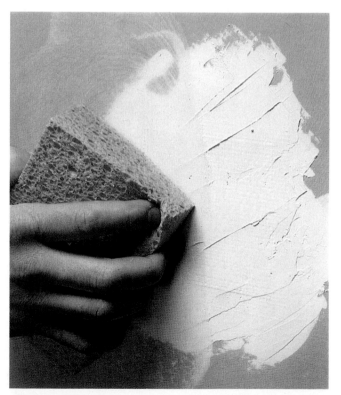

3 Use wallboard knife to cover patch with spackle or wallboard compound. Two coats may be needed. Let patch set until nearly dry.

4 Use a damp sponge or wallboard wet sander to smooth the repair area. This eliminates dust caused by dry sanding.

How to Patch Larger Holes in Wallboard

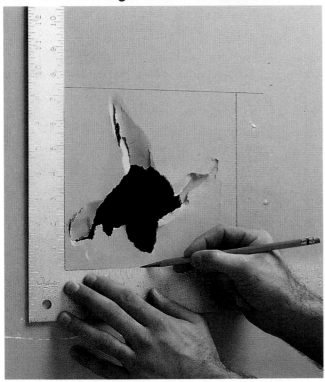

1 Outline the damaged area with a carpenter's square. Use a wallboard saw or jig saw to cut away the damaged section.

2 Install wood or wallboard backer strips. For wood, use a wallboard screw gun and 1¼" wallboard screws to secure the strip in place.

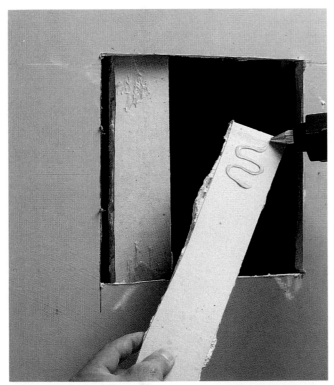

3 Or, use wallboard backers secured by hot glue as an alternative to wood backer strips. Screw or glue wallboard patch in place over backer strips.

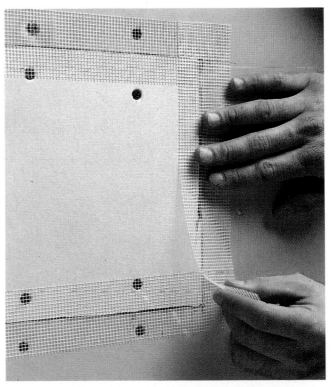

4 Apply wallboard tape to the cracks, then apply wallboard compound and sand the area (page opposite).

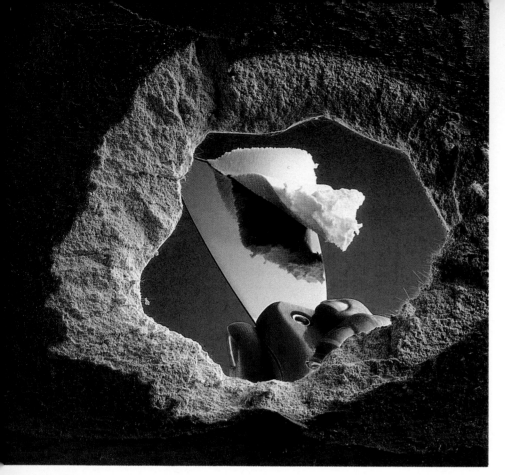

Repairing Holes in Plaster

Modern repair methods and materials have simplified the job of repairing holes in plaster. Coating the patch area with latex bonding liquid ensures a good bond and a tight, crack-free patch. Bonding liquid also eliminates the need to wet the plaster and lath to prevent premature drying and shrinkage. Ask your hardware dealer for a good concrete/plaster latex bonding liquid.

How to Repair Holes in Plaster

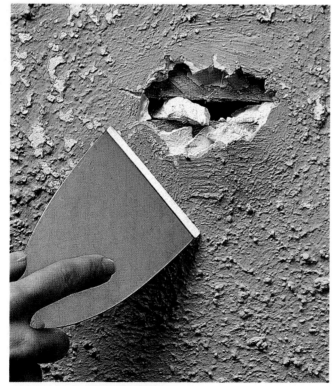

1 Sand or scrape any textured paint from the area around the hole.

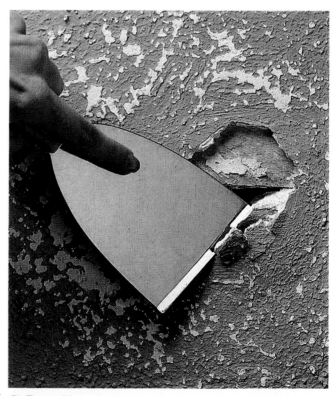

2 Test with a scraper to be sure plaster is solid and tight around the damaged area. Scrape away any loose or soft plaster.

3 Apply latex bonding liquid liberally around edges of hole and over base lath to ensure crack-free bond between old and new plaster.

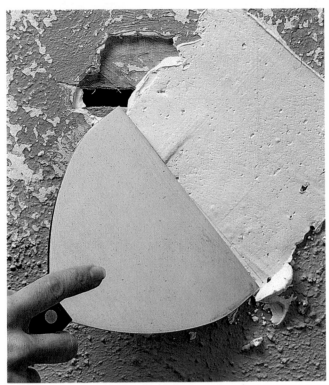

4 Mix patching plaster as directed by manufacturer, and use a wallboard knife or trowel to apply it to the hole. Fill shallow holes with a single coat of plaster.

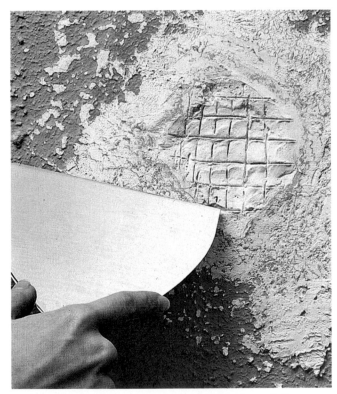

5 For deeper holes, apply shallow first coat, then scratch crosshatch pattern in wet plaster. Let dry, then apply second coat of plaster. Let dry, and sand lightly.

Use texture paint or wallboard compound to recreate any surface texture, as directed on pages 84-85.

Preparing Woodwork

How to Remove Paint with Chemical Stripper

Before painting or refinishing, wood should be cleaned, repaired and sanded. If the old paint is heavily layered or badly chipped, it should be stripped before the wood is repainted.

If using a heat gun to strip wood, take care not to scorch the wood. Never use a heat gun after using chemical strippers: the chemical residue may be vaporized or ignited by the heat.

When using a chemical paint stripper, always wear protective clothing and safety gear, including eye protection and a respirator. Follow the label directions for safe use, and always work in a well-ventilated area.

1 Follow label directions for safe use of chemicals. Wear heavy rubber gloves and eye protection, use drop cloths, and open windows and doors for ventilation when using chemical strippers.

How to Remove Paint with a Heat Gun

1 Hold heat gun near wood until paint softens and just begins to blister. Overheating can make the paint gummy, and may scorch the wood. Always be careful when using a heat gun around flammable materials.

2 Remove softened paint with a scraper or putty knife. Scrapers are available in many shapes for removing paint from shaped moldings. Sand away any paint residue remaining after heat stripping.

2 Apply a liberal coat of stripper to painted wood with a paint brush or steel wool. Let it stand until paint begins to blister. Do not let stripper dry out on wood surfaces.

3 Scrape away paint with a putty knife or scraper and steel wool as soon as it softens. Rub stripped wood with denatured alcohol and new steel wool to help clean grain. Wipe wood with a wet sponge or solvent, as directed on stripper label.

Cleaning & Patching Woodwork

For the best results, woodwork should be cleaned, patched and sanded before it is repainted. A liquid deglosser helps to dull shiny surfaces so they will bond with new paint. If new hardware is to be installed, check to see if new pieces will fit old screw holes. If new screw holes must be drilled, fill the old holes with wood patch.

To renew varnished wood, clean the surfaces with mineral spirits or furniture refinisher, then patch holes with a wood patcher that is tinted to match the existing finish. Sand wood smooth, and apply one or two coats of varnish.

How to Prepare Woodwork for Painting

1 Wash woodwork with TSP solution, and rinse. Scrape away any peeling or loose paint. Badly chipped woodwork should be stripped (pages 52-53).

How to Prepare Varnished Wood for Refinishing

1 Clean woodwork with a soft cloth and odorless mineral spirits or liquid furniture refinisher.

2 Use a putty knife to apply latex wood patch or spackle to any nail holes, dents, and to any other damaged areas.

3 Sand surfaces with 150-grit production paper until they are smooth to the touch. Wipe woodwork with a tack cloth before priming and painting.

2 Apply wood patch to holes and dents with putty knife. Sand patch areas lightly with 150-grit production sandpaper.

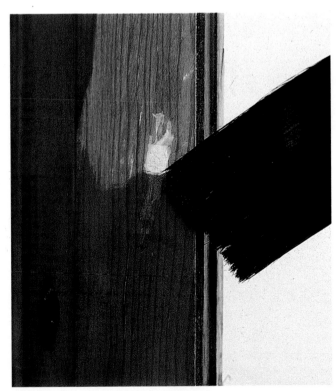

3 Restain the patch areas to match surrounding wood. Apply 1 or 2 coats of varnish (page 80).

Masking & Draping

For fast, mess-free painting, shield any surfaces that could get splattered. If painting only the ceiling, drape the walls and woodwork to prevent splatters. When painting walls, mask the baseboards and the window and door casings.

Remove lightweight furniture, and move heavier pieces to the center of the room and cover with plastic. Cover the floors with 9-ounce canvas drop cloths that will absorb paint splatters.

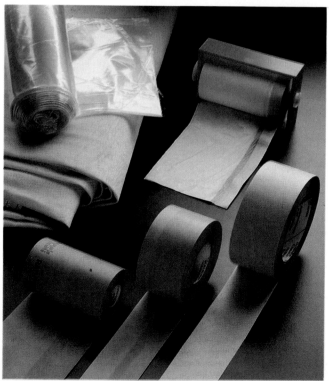

Masking & draping materials, clockwise from top left: plastic and canvas drop cloths, self-adhesive plastic, masking tape, pregummed masking papers. Plastic-paper laminates are also available.

How to Drape Walls

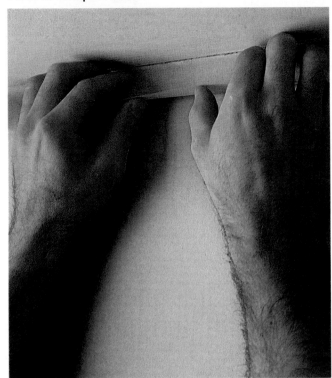

1 Press top half of 2" masking tape along ceiling-wall corners. Leave bottom half of tape loose.

2 Hang sheet plastic under masking tape, draping walls and baseboards. Remove loose edge as soon as the paint is too dry to run.

How to Mask Wood Trim

1 Use pregummed paper or wide masking tape to protect wood moldings from paint splatters. Leave outside edge of masking tape loose.

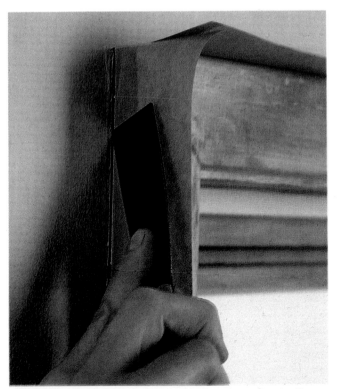

2 After applying tape, run the tip of a putty knife along inside edge of tape to seal against seeping paint. Remove masking material as soon as paint is too dry to run.

Final Check & Cleanup Tips

Before painting, make a final check of the work area. Clean the room thoroughly to eliminate dust that might collect on tools and settle on wet paint. Maintain the temperature and humidity levels recommended by product labels. This will help keep paint edges wet while painting, to avoid lap marks in the finished job.

It is also important for the paint to dry within normal time limits so dirt can't settle on the finish while it is wet. When applying wallcovering, a proper work climate prevents premature drying of the adhesive, and blisters or loose edges on the wallcovering.

Check all surfaces to be painted with a strong side-light. Sand, or spackle and sand, any rough spots that were missed in preparation.

Turn off thermostats for forced air furnaces and air-conditioners so that the fan will not circulate dust through the area being painted.

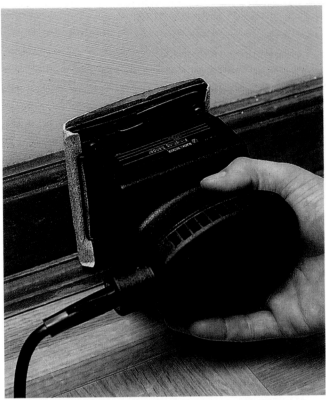

Sand all surfaces that will be painted with 150-grit production sandpaper. Sanding dulls the surface so it will accept new paint. Wipe walls with tack rag.

Wipe dust from woodwork with a tack rag, or with a clean cloth and liquid deglosser.

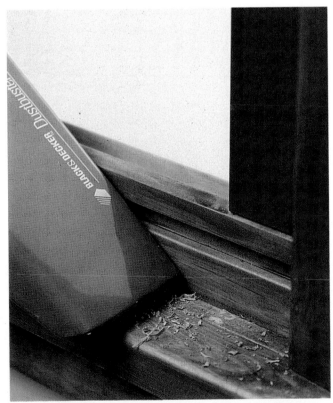

Use a vacuum cleaner to pick up the dust from windowsills and window tracks, and from baseboards and casements.

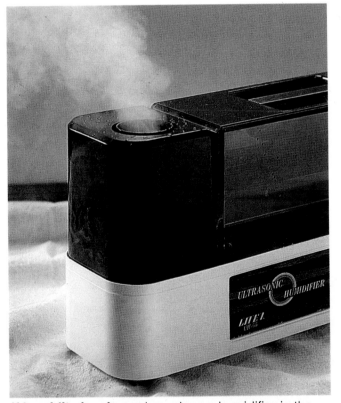

If humidity levels are low, place a humidifier in the room before painting or wallcovering. This keeps paint or adhesive from drying too fast.

Applying Primers & Sealers

A sealer should be applied to wood surfaces before they are varnished. Wood often has both hard and soft grains, as well as a highly absorbent end grain. Applying a sealer helps close the wood surface so that varnish is absorbed evenly in different types of wood grain. If the wood is not sealed, the varnish may dry to a mottled finish.

Primers are used to seal surfaces that will be painted. Wallboard seams and patch areas that have been treated with wallboard compound or patching material can absorb paint at a different rate than the surrounding areas. Joints and patch areas often show or "shadow" through the finished paint if the walls were not adequately primed.

Tint primer with color base available at paint dealers, or request that your dealer tint the primer. A color-matched primer provides an excellent base for finish coat paints.

How to Prime & Seal Before Painting

Seal raw wood by applying a primer before painting or a clear sealer before varnishing. Unsealed wood can produce a spotty finish.

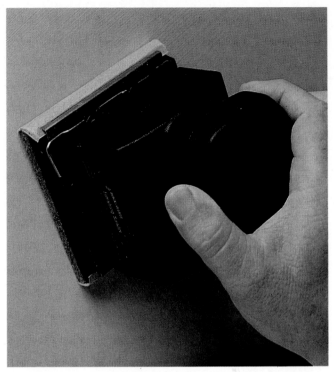

Roughen gloss surfaces with fine sandpaper, then prime to provide good bonding between the new and the old paint. Primers provide "tooth" for the new coat of paint.

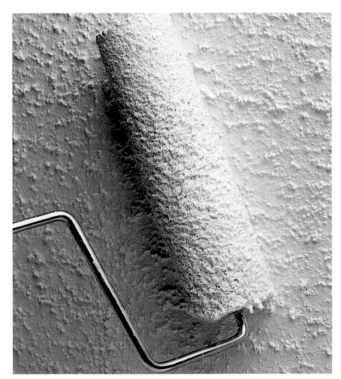

Seal textured surfaces with a PVA or alkyd primer, then apply finish coat with a long-nap roller. Textured walls and ceilings soak up a lot of paint and make it difficult to apply paint evenly.

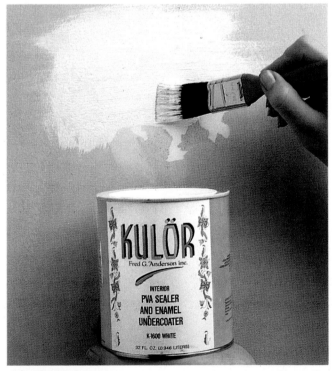

Spot-prime minor repair areas on plaster or wallboard with PVA primer.

Painting

Painting Safety

Always read and follow the label information on paint and solvent containers. Chemicals that pose a fire hazard are listed (in order of flammability) as: combustible, flammable, or extremely flammable. Use caution when using these products, and remember that the fumes are also flammable.

The warning "use with adequate ventilation" means that there should be no more vapor buildup than there would be if using the material outside. Open doors and windows, use exhaust fans and an approved safety mask if you can smell paint or solvent.

Paint chemicals do not store well. Buy just as much as is needed for the project and keep chemicals away from children. Use up excess paint by applying an extra coat or follow local guidelines regarding paint disposal.

Read label information. Chemicals that are poisonous or flammable are labeled with warnings and instructions for safe handling.

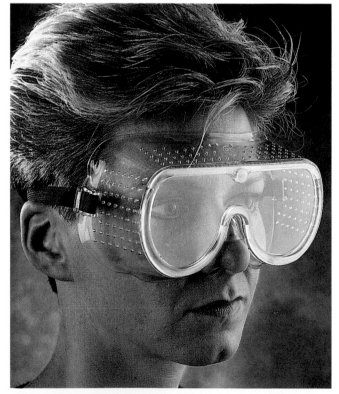

Wear safety goggles when using chemical stripper or cleaning products. Use goggles when painting overhead.

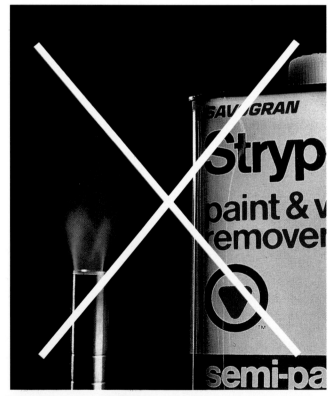

Do not use chemicals that are listed as combustible or flammable, such as paint strippers, near an open flame. Appliance pilot lights can ignite chemical vapors.

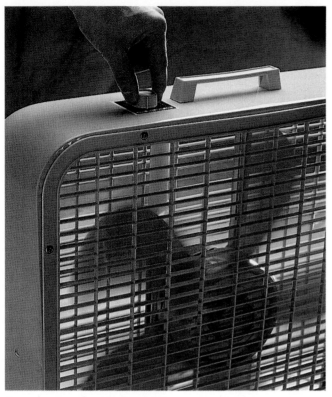

Open windows and doors and use a fan for ventilation when painting indoors. If a product label has the warning "harmful or fatal if swallowed," assume that the vapors are dangerous to breathe.

Use an approved mask to filter vapors if you cannot ventilate a work area properly. If you can smell vapors, the ventilation is not adequate.

Let thinners stand after cleaning tools. After the solid material settles out, pour off the clear thinner and save for reuse. Discard sediment.

Dispose of leftover paint safely. Let container stand uncovered until solvent evaporates, then re-cover and dispose of the container with other trash.

Choosing Paint

Paints are either water-base latex or alkyd-base. **Latex paint** is easy to apply and clean up, and the improved chemistry of today's latexes makes them suitable for nearly every application. Some painters feel that **alkyd paint** allows for a smoother finished surface, but local regulations may restrict the use of alkyd-base products.

Paints come in various sheens. Paint finishes range from flat to high-gloss enamels. Gloss enamels dry to a shiny finish, and are used for surfaces that will be washed often, like bathrooms, kitchens and woodwork. Flat paints are used for most wall and ceiling applications.

Always use a good primer to coat surfaces before painting. The primer bonds well to all surfaces, and provides a durable base that keeps the finish coat from cracking or peeling. Tint the primer to match the new color to avoid the need for a second coat of expensive finish paint.

How to Estimate Paint

1) Length of wall or ceiling (feet)	
2) Height of wall, or width of ceiling	×
3) Surface area	=
4) Coverage per gallon of chosen paint	÷
5) **Gallons of paint needed**	=

How to Select a Quality Paint

Paint coverage listed on label of quality paint should be about 400 square feet per gallon. Bargain paints (left) may require 2 or even 3 coats to cover the same area.

High washability is a feature of quality paint. The pigments in bargain paints (right) may "chalk" and wash away with mild scrubbing.

Paint Sheens

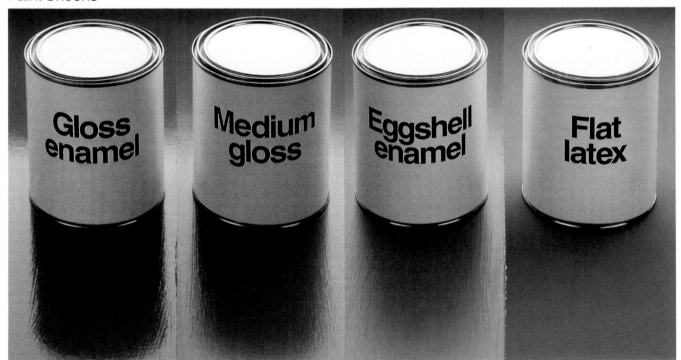

Range of sheens, from left: **Gloss enamel,** a highly reflective finish for areas where high washability is important. All gloss paints tend to show surface flaws. Alkyd-base enamels have highest gloss. **Medium-gloss** latex enamel, a highly washable surface with a slightly less reflective finish. Like gloss enamels, medium-gloss paints tend to show surface flaws. **Eggshell enamel,** combining soft finish with the washability of enamel. **Flat latex,** an all-purpose paint with a soft finish that hides surface irregularities.

Work light

⅜'' nap roller

Paint tray

3'' paintbrush

2'' trim brush

Tapered sash brush

Painting Tools & Equipment

Most painting jobs can be done with a few quality tools. Purchase two or three premium brushes, a sturdy paint pan that can be attached to a stepladder, and one or two good rollers. With proper cleanup, these tools will last for years.

Brushes made of hog or ox bristles should be used only with alkyd-base paints. All-purpose brushes blend polyester, nylon, and sometimes animal bristles. Choose a straight-edged 3" wall brush, a 2" straight-edged trim brush, and a tapered sash brush.

How to Choose a Paintbrush

Hardwood handle

Reinforced ferrule

Spacer plugs

Flagged bristles

Chiseled end

3" Straight brush

2" Trim brush

Tapered sash brush

Quality brush, shown in left cutaway, has shaped hardwood handle and a sturdy reinforced ferrule made of noncorrosive metal. Multiple spacer plugs separate bristles. Quality brush has flagged (split) bristles and a chiseled end for precise edging. A cheaper brush will have a blunt end, unflagged bristles and a cardboard spacer plug that may soften when wet.

3" straight-edged brush (top) is a good choice for cutting paint lines at ceilings and in corners. For painting woodwork, a 2" trim brush (middle) works well. Choose brushes with chiseled tips for painting in corners. A tapered sash brush (bottom) may help when painting corners on window sashes.

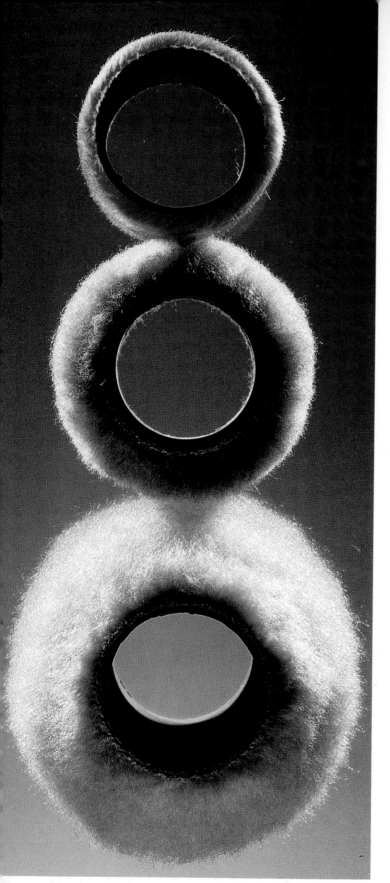

Choosing Rollers & Roller Accessories

A good paint roller is an inexpensive, timesaving tool that can last for years. Choose a standard 9-inch roller with a wire frame and nylon bearings. The roller should feel well balanced, and should have a handle molded to fit your hand. The handle should also have a threaded end that lets you attach an extension for painting ceilings and high walls.

Roller covers are available in a wide variety of nap lengths, but most jobs can be done with ⅜" nap. Select medium-priced **synthetic** roller covers that can be reused a few times before discarding. Bargain roller covers might shed fibers onto the painted surface, and cannot be cleaned and reused. Rinse all roller covers in solvent to prevent lint.

Use more expensive **lamb's wool** roller covers when using most alkyd-base paints. **Mohair** covers work well with gloss alkyd paints where complete smoothness is important.

Nap length. Select proper roller cover for the surface you intend to paint. ¼"-nap covers (top) are used for very flat surfaces. ⅜"-nap covers (middle) will cover the small flaws found in most flat walls and ceilings. 1"-nap covers (bottom) fill spaces in rough surfaces, like concrete blocks or stucco walls.

Cover material. Synthetic covers (left) are good with most paints, especially latexes. Wool or mohair roller covers (right) give an even finish with alkyd products. Choose better quality roller covers that do not shed lint.

Choose sturdy roller handle with wire cage construction. Nylon bearings should roll smoothly and easily when you spin the cage. The handle end should be threaded for attaching an extension handle.

Buy paint tray with legs that allow the tray to sit steadily on the shelf of a stepladder. A good paint tray will resist flexing when it is twisted. Look for a textured ramp that keeps the roller turning easily.

Five-gallon paint container and paint screen speeds painting of large areas. Load paint roller straight from bucket, using a roller extension handle. Do not try to balance pail on stepladder shelf.

Use a 4-foot extension handle to paint ceilings and walls easily without a ladder.

Special Painting Tools

Airless paint sprayer is useful for painting large areas, or for irregular surfaces like louvered closet doors or heat registers. All sprayers produce some overspray, so wear protective gear and mask off all areas likely to be splattered. Movable workpieces should be painted outside or in your basement or garage. Thinning the paint before spraying will result in easier use of the tool and more even coverage.

Surfaces with unusual angles and contours are sometimes difficult to paint with standard rollers and brushes. Specialty tools make some painting situations easier. Disposable foam brushes, for instance, are excellent for applying an even coat of clear varnish to smooth woodwork.

Specialty rollers & pads come in various shapes for painting edges, corners, and other unique applications.

Bendable tool can be shaped to fit unusual surfaces, such as window shutters or the fins of cast-iron radiators.

Paint glove simplifies painting of pipes and other contoured surfaces, like wrought-iron.

Paint pads and specialty rollers come in a wide range of sizes and shapes to fit different painting needs.

Aerosol spray paint speeds painting of any small, intricate job, like painting heat registers.

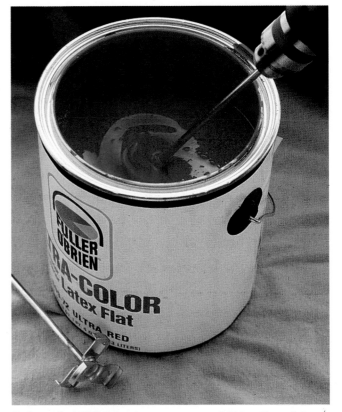

Paint mixer bit attaches to power drill to stir paints quickly and easily. Use variable-speed drill at low speed to avoid air bubbles in paint.

Mix paint together (called "boxing") in a large pail to eliminate slight color variations between cans. Stir the paint thoroughly with a wooden stick or power drill attachment. Keep paint from building up in the groove around the paint can lid. Pound several small nail holes into the groove to let paint drip back into the can.

Basic Painting Techniques

For a professional-looking paint job, paint must be spread evenly onto the work surfaces without running, dripping or lapping onto other areas. Excess paint will run on the surface and can drip onto woodwork and floors. Stretching paint too far leaves lap marks and causes incomplete coverage.

Painting with brushes and rollers is a three-step process. Paint is first applied, is next distributed evenly, and is finally smoothed out for an even finish.

How to Use a Paint Brush

1 Dip the brush, loading one-third of bristle length. Tap the bristles against the side of the can. Dipping deeper overloads the brush. Dragging the brush against the lip of the can causes the bristles to wear.

2 Cut in edges using narrow edge of brush, pressing just enough to flex the bristles. Keep an eye on the paint edge, and paint with long slow strokes. Always paint from dry area back into wet paint to avoid lap marks.

3 Brush wall corners using wide edge of brush. Paint open areas with brush or roller before brushed paint dries.

4 To paint large areas with a brush, apply paint with 2 or 3 diagonal strokes. Hold brush at about 45° angle to work surface, pressing just enough to flex bristles. Distribute paint evenly with horizontal strokes.

5 Smooth off surface by drawing brush vertically from top to bottom of painted area. Use light strokes and lift the brush from the surface at end of each stroke. This method is best for slow-drying alkyd enamels.

Using a Paint Roller

Paint surfaces in small sections, working from dry surfaces back into wet paint to avoid roller marks. If a paint job takes more than a day, cover the roller tightly with plastic wrap or store it in a bucket of water overnight to prevent paint from drying out.

1 Wet the roller cover with water (when painting with latex paint) or mineral spirits (when painting with alkyd enamel), to remove lint and prime the roller cover. Squeeze out excess solvent. Fill the paint tray reservoir. Dip roller fully into reservoir to load paint.

3 With the loaded roller, make a diagonal sweep (1) about 4' long on surface. On walls, roll upward on the first stroke to avoid spilling paint. Use slow roller strokes to avoid splattering.

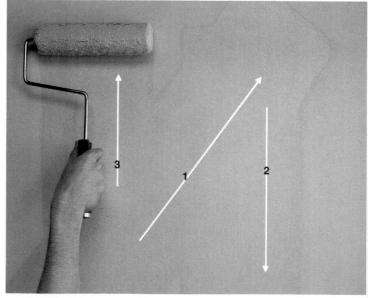

4 Draw roller straight down (2) from top of diagonal sweep. Move roller to beginning of diagonal and roll up (3) to complete unloading of roller.

2 Lift the roller from the paint reservoir, and roll back-and-forth on the textured ramp to distribute the paint evenly on the nap. Roller should be full but not dripping when lifted from the paint pan.

5 Distribute paint over section with horizontal back-and-forth strokes.

6 Smooth off area by lightly drawing roller vertically from top to bottom of painted area. Lift roller and return it to top of area after each stroke.

Painting Trim

When painting an entire room, paint the wood trim first, then the walls. Start by painting the inside portions of trim and working out toward walls. On windows, for instance, first paint the edges close to the glass, then the surrounding face trim.

Doors should be painted quickly because of the large surface. To avoid lap marks, always paint from dry surfaces back into wet paint. On baseboards, cut in the top edge and work down to the flooring. Plastic floor guards or a wide broadknife can help shield carpet and wood flooring from paint drips.

Alkyds and latex enamels may require two coats. Always sand lightly between coats and wipe with a tack cloth so that the second coat bonds properly.

How to Paint a Window

1 To paint double-hung windows, remove them from frames, if possible. Newer, spring-mounted windows are released by pushing against the frame (arrow).

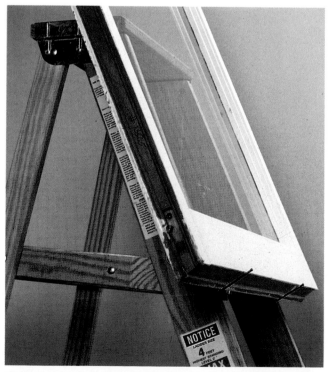

2 Drill holes and insert 2 nails into the legs of wooden stepladder, and mount the window easel-style for easy painting; or lay window flat on bench or sawhorses. Do not paint sides or bottom of sashes.

3 Using a tapered sash brush, begin by painting the wood next to the glass. Use narrow edge of brush, and overlap paint onto the glass to create a weatherseal.

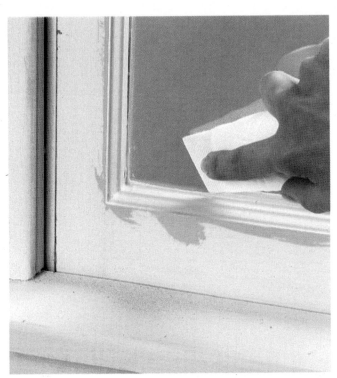

4 Clean excess paint off glass with a putty knife wrapped in a clean cloth. Rewrap the knife often so that you always wipe with clean fabric. Leave 1/16" paint overlap from sash onto glass.

Case molding

Sash

Sill

Apron

5 Paint flat portions of sashes (1), then the case moldings (2), sill (3) and apron (4). Use slow brush strokes, and avoid getting paint between sash and frame.

6 If you must paint windows in place, move the painted windows up and down several times during the drying period to keep them from sticking. Use putty knife to avoid touching painted surface.

How to Paint Doors

1 Remove the door by driving lower hinge pin out with a screwdriver and hammer. Have a helper hold door in place. Drive out the upper hinge pin.

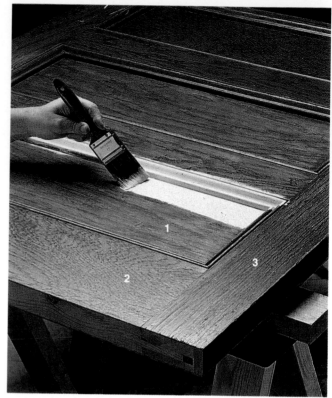

2 Place the door flat on sawhorses to paint. On paneled doors, paint in the following order: 1) recessed panels, 2) horizontal rails, and 3) vertical stiles.

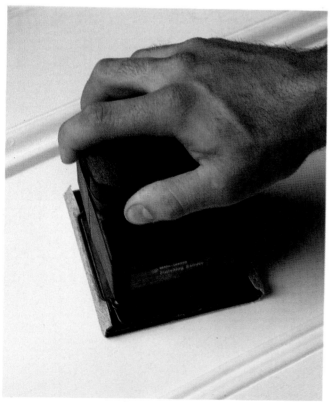

3 Let door dry. If a second coat of paint is needed, sand lightly and wipe the door with tack cloth before repainting.

4 Seal the unpainted edges of the door with clear wood sealer to prevent moisture from entering wood. Water can cause wood to warp and swell.

Tips for Painting Trim

Protect wall and floor surfaces with a wide broad-knife, or with plastic shielding tool.

Wipe paint off of broadknife or shielding tool each time it is moved.

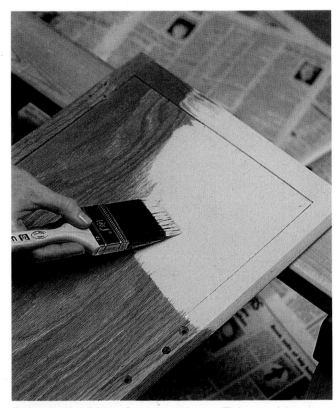

Paint both sides of cabinet doors. This provides an even moisture seal and prevents warping.

Paint deep patterned surfaces with a stiff-bristled brush, like this stenciling brush. Use small circular strokes to penetrate recesses.

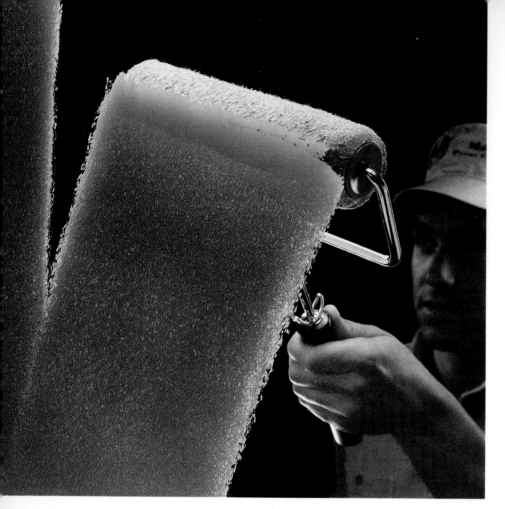

Painting Ceilings & Walls

For a smooth finish on large wall and ceiling areas, paint in small sections. First use a paintbrush to cut in the edge, then immediately roll the section before moving on. If brushed edges are left to dry before the large surfaces are rolled, visible lap marks will be left on the finished wall. Working in natural light makes it easier to spot missed areas.

Choose quality paint and tools, and work with a full brush or roller to avoid lap marks and assure full coverage. Keep roller speed slow to minimize paint splattering.

Tips for Painting Ceilings & Walls

Paint to a wet edge. Cut in edge on small section with a paintbrush just before rolling, then move on to next section. With two painters, let one cut in with a brush while the other rolls large areas.

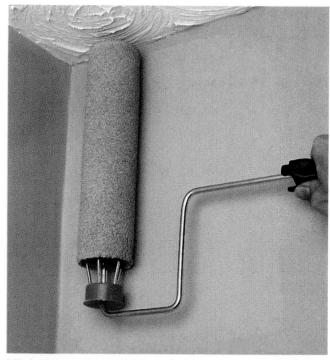

Minimize brush marks. Slide roller cover slightly off when rolling near ceiling line or wall corners. Brushed areas dry to a different finish than rolled paint.

How to Paint Ceilings

Paint ceilings with a roller handle extension. Use eye protection while painting overhead. Start at the corner farthest from the entry door. Paint the ceiling along the narrow end in 3×3' sections, cutting in the edges with a brush before rolling. Apply paint with diagonal stroke. Distribute paint evenly with back-and-forth strokes. For the final smoothing strokes, roll each section toward the entry wall, lifting the roller at the end of each sweep.

How to Paint Walls

Paint walls in 2×4' sections. Start in an upper corner, cutting in ceiling and wall corners with a brush, then rolling the section. Make initial diagonal stroke of roller from bottom of section upward, to avoid dripping paint. Distribute paint evenly with horizontal strokes, then finish with downward sweeps of the roller. Next, cut in and roll the section directly underneath. Continue with adjacent areas, cutting in and rolling top sections before bottom. All finish strokes should be rolled toward the floor.

Texture Painting

Texture paints offer a decorating alternative to either flat paints or wallcoverings. The variety of possible effects you can achieve is limited only by your imagination. Texture paints are available in either premixed latex formulations or in dry powder form. Premixed latex texture paints are fine for producing light stipple patterns, but powder textures are a better choice for creating heavier adobe or stucco finishes. Powder textures are available in 25-lb. bags, and must be mixed with water, using a paint mixer bit and power drill.

Practice textures on heavy cardboard until you get the pattern you want. Remember that the depth of the texture depends on the stiffness of the texture paint, the amount applied to the surface and the type of tool used to create the texture.

How to Texture Paint

Create swirl pattern with whisk broom. Apply the texture paint with a roller, then use broom to achieve the design wanted.

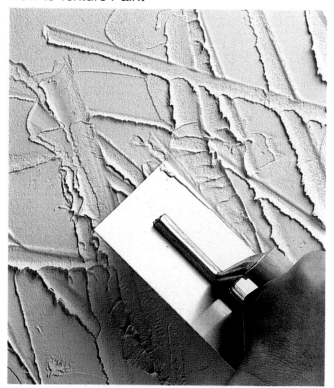

Trowel texture material onto the surface, and pile the material in ridges to create an adobe pattern.

Dab, drag or swirl a sponge through texture paint to create an endless variety of texture patterns. Or, let the first course dry, then sponge another color on top for a two-tone stucco effect.

Use long-nap roller to make this stipple texture effect. For different patterns, vary the pressure on the roller and amount of texture paint on the surface.

Create crowsfoot design by applying texture paint with a roller, brushing it out level, then randomly striking the surface with the flat of the brush.

Press the flat side of a trowel into texture paint and pull it away to create a stomp design.

Trowel over texture pattern when the paint has partially dried, to flatten peaks and achieve a brocade design. Clean trowel between strokes with a wet brush or sponge.

Cleaning Up

At the end of a paint job you may choose to throw away the roller covers, but the paint pans, roller handles and brushes can be cleaned and stored for future use. Stray paint drips can be wiped away if they are still wet. A putty knife or razor will remove many dried paint spots on hardwood or glass. Remove stubborn paint from most surfaces with a chemical cleaner.

Cleaning products, from left: chemical cleaner, spinner tool, cleaner tool for brushes and roller covers.

Use spinner tool to remove paint and solvent. Wash the roller cover or brush with solvent, then attach to the spinner. Pumping the handle throws liquids out of the roller cover or brush. Hold the spinner inside a cardboard box or 5-gallon pail to catch paint and avoid splatters.

Cleanup Tips

Comb brush bristles with spiked side of cleaner tool. This aligns the bristles so they dry properly.

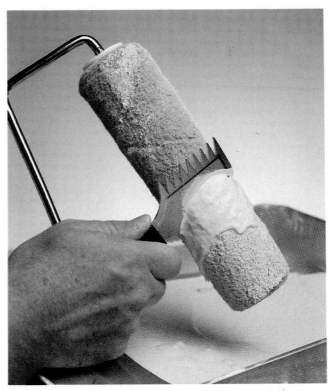

Scrape paint from roller cover with curved side of cleaner tool. Remove as much paint as possible before washing tools with solvent.

Store brushes in their original wrappers, or fold the bristles inside brown wrapping paper. Store washed roller covers on end to avoid flattening the nap.

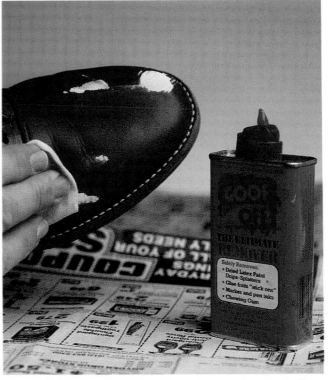

Remove dried splatters with a chemical cleaner. Before using cleaner, test an inconspicuous area to make sure surface is colorfast.

Wallcovering

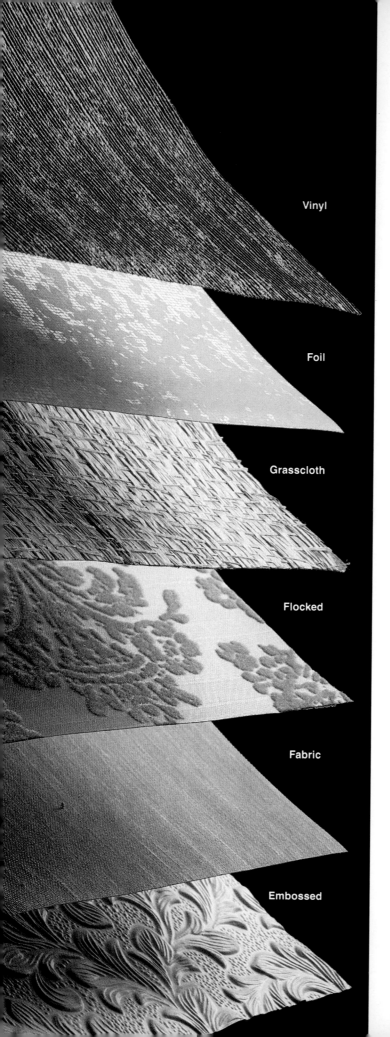

Vinyl

Foil

Grasscloth

Flocked

Fabric

Embossed

Choosing the Right Wallcovering

Very few modern "wallpapers" are actually made of paper. Today's wallcoverings may be made of vinyl, vinyl-coated paper or cloth, textiles, natural grasses, foil or mylar. Vinyl or coated vinyl coverings are the easiest to hang, clean and remove. Other types of wallcoverings can give a room a unique look, but may require special handling. Your choice of wallcovering depends on the needs of the room and on your confidence and ability.

Types of Wallcovering

Vinyl wallcoverings are made with a continuous flexible film, often applied over a fabric or paper backing. Some vinyls successfully duplicate the effect of natural grasscloth or textile wallcoverings. Because they are easy to apply, clean and remove, vinyl wallcoverings with preapplied adhesives are a good choice.

Foils or mylars are coated with a thin, flexible metallic film. These highly reflective wallcoverings add brightness to any room, but they require careful handling. Foils also reveal all wall flaws, so surface preparation must be perfect.

Grasscloths are imported wallcoverings that use natural plant fibers. Because they reflect little light, grasscloths soften the appearance of a room. They are a good choice for flawed, irregular walls. Hang them with clear adhesive. Never use water to rinse grasscloths.

Flocked wallcoverings are patterned with raised fibers that suggest the look of velvet. Avoid heavy brushing when hanging flocked wallcoverings, and never use a seam roller.

Fabric wallcoverings are made of woven textiles. Fabrics are easy to hang because there is no pattern to match, but they may be difficult to clean.

Embossed wallcoverings are stamped with a relief pattern for an elegant, formal appearance. Never use a seam roller on embossed wallpapers: they can be easily damaged.

Tips for Choosing Wallcovering

Removability: Strippable wallcoverings (left) can be pulled away from the wall by hand leaving little or no film or residue. Peelable wallcoverings (right) can be removed, but may leave a thin paper layer on the wall, which can usually be removed with soap and water. Check the back of the sample or the wallcovering package for its strippability rating. Choose a strippable product to make future redecorating easier.

Washability: Washable wallcoverings can be cleaned with mild soap and water and a sponge. Scrubbable wallcoverings are durable enough to be scrubbed with a soft brush. Choose scrubbable wallcoverings for any heavy-use areas.

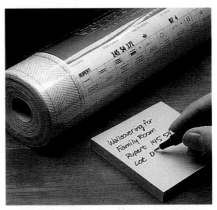

Application: Prepasted wallcoverings (left) are factory-coated with water-base adhesive that is activated when wallcovering is wetted in a water tray. Unpasted wallcoverings (right) must be coated with an adhesive for hanging. As well as being easier to prepare, today's prepasted products are just as durable as those requiring an adhesive coat.

Dye-lot: Jot down dye-lot numbers for reference. If you need additional rolls, order from the same dye-lot to avoid slight color differences.

Packaging: Wallcoverings are sold in continuous triple, double and single-roll bolts.

Patterns: There is always more waste with large patterns. A wallcovering with a large drop pattern can be more expensive to hang than one with a smaller repeat. With large designs, it may also be difficult to avoid obvious pattern interruptions at baseboards or corners.

Measuring & Estimating Wallcovering

With a few room measurements, and the information listed on the wallcovering package, you can estimate the correct amount of wallcovering to buy. The procedure given on these two pages will help you calculate the square footage of your walls and ceilings, and show you how to find the per-roll coverage of wallcovering.

Because of normal trimming waste, the per-roll coverage of wallcovering will be at least 15% less than the coverage listed on the package. The waste percentage can be higher depending on how much space it takes for the wallcovering pattern to repeat itself. This "pattern repeat" measurement is listed on the wallcovering package. You can compensate for this extra waste factor by adding the pattern repeat measurement to the wall height measurement of the room.

Measure the room: Walls: Measure the **length** of the wall, to the nearest ½ foot. (Add length of all walls to find the **perimeter**, if entire room will be wallcovered.) Include window and door openings in wall measurements. Measure the **height** of surfaces to be covered, to nearest ½ foot. Do not include baseboards or crown moldings in height measurement. **Ceilings:** Measure the **length** and the **width** of the ceiling to the nearest ½ foot.

How to Measure Unusual Surfaces

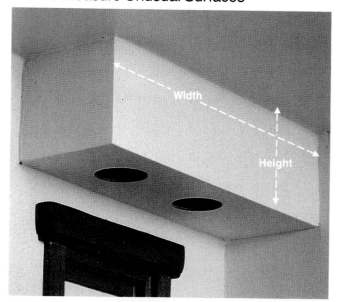

Soffits. If covering all sides of a soffit, add the **width** and **height** into the wall or ceiling measurement.

Triangular walls. Measure as though surface is square: length × height.

How to Figure Actual Per-roll Coverage

1) Total per-roll coverage (square feet)	
2) Adjust for waste factor	× .85
3) **Actual Per-roll Coverage** (square feet)	=

How to Calculate Rolls Needed for a Ceiling

1) Room length (feet)	
2) Wallcovering pattern repeat (feet)	+
3) Adjusted length (feet)	=
4) Room width (feet)	×
5) Ceiling area (square feet)	=
6) Actual Per-roll Coverage (figured above; square feet)	÷
7) **Number of Rolls Needed for Ceiling**	=

How to Calculate Rolls Needed for Walls

1) Wall height (feet)	
2) Wallcovering pattern repeat (feet)	+
3) Adjusted height (feet)	=
4) Wall length; or room perimeter (feet)	×
5) Wall area (square feet)	=
6) Actual Per-roll Coverage (figured above; square feet)	÷
7) Number of rolls	=
8) Add 1 roll for each archway or recessed window	+
9) **Number of Rolls Needed for Walls**	=

Wallcovering package or pattern book gives per-roll coverage in square feet, and the drop pattern repeat measurement.

Paint pail

Natural sponge

Water tray

Paint tray & roller

Bubblestick

Smoothing brushes

Smoothing tool

Broadknife

Seam roller

Razor knife

Wallcovering scissors

Tools for Wallcovering

Many of the tools for hanging wallcovering are common items you may already have. Keep a supply of #2 pencils and a pencil sharpener handy for precise marking when laying out and cutting wallcovering. Never use an ink marker or ballpoint pen, because the ink might bleed through the wet wallcovering.

Use a bubblestick or carpenter's level for establishing plumb lines and as a straightedge for cutting. Don't use a chalkline: the chalk can smear the new wallcovering or ooze through the seams. Trim wallcoverings with a razor knife that features breakaway tips. Buy noncorrosive paint pails for holding wash water, and use a natural or high-quality plastic sponge to avoid damaging the wallcovering.

Wallcovering adhesives can be applied with an ordinary paint roller, but you will need a smoothing tool to flatten the wallcovering strips as you hang them, and a seam roller to fix the joints between strips. Ask your dealer about the proper tools for your wallcovering.

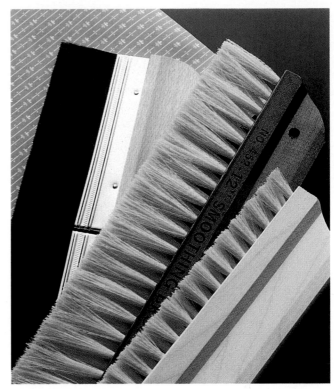

Smoothing brushes come in various nap lengths. Use a short nap brush for smoothing out vinyl wallcoverings. A soft, long nap brush is used for fragile wallcoverings, like flocks and grasscloths.

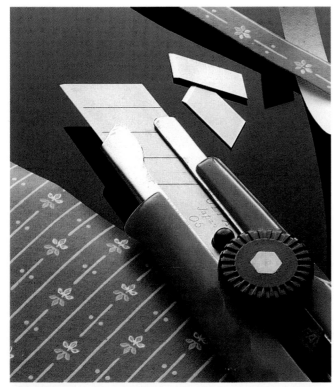

Razor knife with breakaway blade is used for trimming wallcovering at ceiling, baseboard, corners, windows and doors. Renew tips often to avoid snagging and tearing wallcovering.

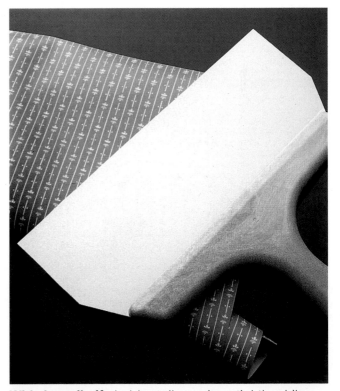

Wide broadknife holds wallcoverings tightly while trimming overlaps in corners and against window or door casings. A narrower broadknife may work better for intricate corners.

(continued next page)

Wallcovering Tools (continued)

Bubblestick or carpenter's level is used to mark verticals for plumb line, and doubles as a straightedge for marking lines. Use a level instead of a chalk line: chalk can bleed through wallcovering seams.

Use wallcovering scissors to trim wallcovering at the seam where wall and ceiling coverings meet. Razor knife may puncture underlying ceiling strip.

Wallcoverer's table provides a flat working surface. Wallcovering stores lend or rent tables, or make your own by placing a sheet of plywood on sawhorses.

Hold a straightedge tightly against the booked wallcovering strip and cut with a sharp razor knife to form partial strips for corners. Hold knife blade straight while cutting the strip.

Wallcovering tray holds water for wetting prepasted wallcover strips.

Sponge and bucket are used for rinsing down strips. Use a natural or quality synthetic sponge.

Paint roller or paste brush is used to apply adhesive to back of unpasted wallcovering strips.

Materials for Wallcovering

Before hanging wallcovering, the wall surfaces must be both sealed and sized to prevent the adhesives from soaking into the wall surface. Today's premixed primer-sealers do both jobs with a single application.

If your wallcovering is not pre-pasted, you will need one or more types of adhesive. For most vinyl or vinyl-backed wallcoverings, choose a heavy-duty premixed vinyl adhesive that contains a mildew inhibitor. Vinyl wallcoverings also require a special vinyl-on-vinyl adhesive for areas where the wallcovering strips overlap, such as around wall corners and archways.

When hanging specialty wallcoverings, you may need special adhesives. Natural grasscloths, for instance, require a clear-drying adhesive that will not soak through and stain the fibers. Check the wallcovering label or ask your dealer about the correct adhesives for your application.

Latex primer-sealer seals and sizes walls in one application. Available as a powder or in premixed form.

Heavy-duty vinyl adhesive is used to hang vinyl or vinyl backed wallcoverings.

Vinyl over vinyl adhesive fastens lap seams on vinyl wallcoverings. Also used to apply vinyl borders over vinyl wallcoverings.

Sketch out seams. Mismatch should be in an inconspicuous area, like behind a door.

The Hanging Plan

Tips for Planning Seams

When hanging any patterned wallcovering, there will be one seam where a full strip meets a partial strip. The pattern will usually mismatch at this point. Plan this mismatched seam in an inconspicuous spot, like behind a door or above an entrance.

Sketch out seam lines before you begin. Avoid placing seams that will be difficult to handle. A seam that falls close to the edge of a window or fireplace complicates the job. At corners, wallcovering should always overlap slightly onto the opposite wall. If one or more seams falls in a bad spot, adjust your plumb line a few inches to compensate.

Plan the mismatch. If the room has no obvious focal point, start at the corner farthest from the entry. Measure out a distance equal to wallcovering width and mark a point. Work in both directions, marking out points where the seams will fall.

Start at focal point, like a fireplace or large window. Center a plumb line on the focal point, then sketch a wall covering plan in both directions from center line.

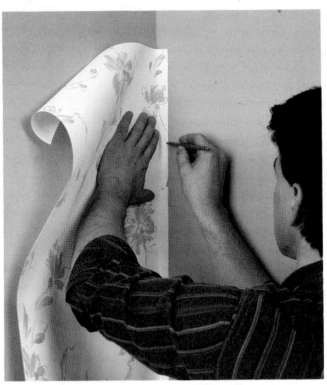

Adjust for corners that fall exactly on seam lines. Make sure you have at least ½" overlap on inside corners, and 1" on outside corners.

Adjust for seams that fall in difficult locations, like near the edge of windows or doors. Shift your starting point so that the seams leave you with workable widths of wallcovering around obstacles.

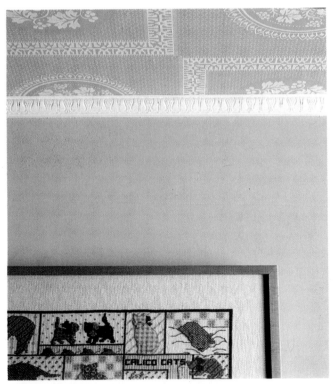

Plan ceiling so that any pattern interruption will be along the least conspicuous side of the room. Pattern interruptions occur on the last ceiling strip, so begin hanging covering opposite the side where the room is entered.

Reroll each wallcovering roll with pattern side in. Inspect the pattern surface for color and design flaws. Return flawed rolls to your dealer.

Basic Wallcovering Handling Techniques

For durability and easy application, choose a quality prepasted vinyl wallcovering whenever possible. Clear the room of all furniture that can be easily removed, and layer newspapers or drop cloths next to the walls. For easy handling, rent a wallcoverer's table, or use any flat, elevated surface. Shut off electricity, and cover outlet receptacle slots with masking tape to keep out water and adhesive. Work during daylight and make sure each strip is perfectly positioned before going on to the next. Have another person help you, especially when covering ceilings.

Tip: Some premium wallcoverings have unprinted side edges (called "selvages") that protect the roll. The selvages must be cut off the wallcovering strip with a razor knife and straightedge before hanging. The selvages may have printed guide marks for precise cutting.

How to Handle Wallcovering Strips

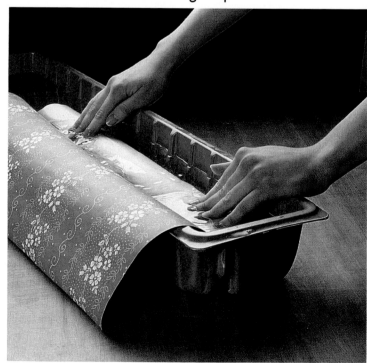

1 Fill water tray half full of lukewarm water. Roll the cut strip loosely with pattern side in. Wet roll in tray as directed by manufacturer, usually about 1 minute.

How to Measure & Cut Wallcovering Strips

1 Hold wallcovering against wall. Make sure there is a full pattern at the ceiling line, and that wallcovering overlaps ceiling and baseboard by about 2''. Cut strip with scissors.

2 For next strips, find the pattern match with the previously hung strip, then measure and cut new strip with about 2'' excess at each end.

How to Handle Unpasted Wallcovering

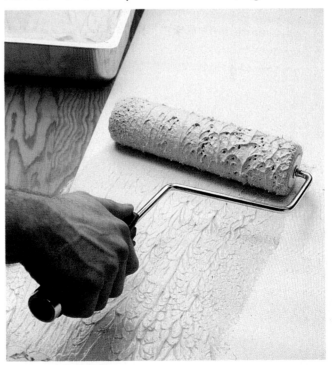

2 Holding one edge of the strip with both hands, lift wallcovering from water. Watch pasted side to make sure strip is evenly wetted. Book strip as indicated (page 102).

Lay strip with pattern side down on wallcoverer's table or a flat surface. Apply adhesive evenly to the strip, using a paint roller. Wipe any adhesive from table before preparing next strip.

How to Book Wallcovering Strips

"Book" wallcovering by folding both ends of the strip to center, with pasted side in. Do not crease the folds. Let strip stand (cure) for about 10 minutes. Some wallcoverings should not be booked: follow the manufacturer's directions.

For ceiling strips or wallcovering borders, use an "accordion" book. Fold strip back and forth with pasted side in for easy handling. Let strip stand (cure) for about 10 minutes.

How to Position & Smooth Wallcovering

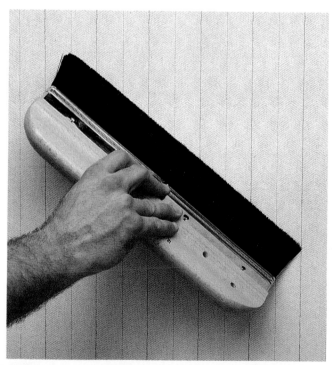

1 Unfold booked strip and position it lightly with edge butted against plumb line or previous strip. Use flat palms to slide strip precisely into place. Flatten top of strip with a smoothing brush.

2 Beginning at top, smooth wallcovering out from center in both directions. Check for bubbles, and make sure seams are properly butted. Pull strip away and reposition if necessary.

How to Trim Wallcovering

1 Hold wallcovering against molding or ceiling with a wide broadknife. Cut away excess with a sharp razor knife. Keep knife blade in place while changing position of broadknife.

2 With wallcovered ceilings, crease the wall strips with broadknife, then cut along crease with scissors. Cutting with razor knife may puncture ceiling strip.

How to Roll Seams

How to Rinse Wallcovering

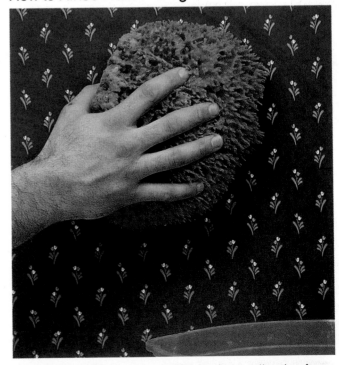

Let strips stand for about ½ hour. Roll seam gently with seam roller. Do not press out adhesive. Do not roll seams on flocks, foils, fabrics or embossed wall-coverings: tap the seams gently with smoothing brush.

Use clear water and a sponge to rinse adhesive from surfaces. Change water after every 3 or 4 strips. Do not let water run along seams. Do not use water on grass-cloths, flocks and fabrics.

Hanging Specialty Wallcoverings

Specialty wallcoverings can add new interest to a room, but most require special handling techniques. Reflective wallcoverings, such as foils and mylars, can add light to even the darkest rooms; but the walls must be perfectly smooth before hanging. Fabric or grasscloth wallcoverings can soften and hide flaws in irregular walls, but they are difficult to keep clean.

For very rough walls, consider hanging a liner paper before the wallcovering. Liner paper strips are hung horizontally so that the wallcovering seams cannot overlap the liner seams.

Always follow the manufacturer's directions when hanging specialty wallcoverings, and make your selection carefully: specialty wallcoverings can be expensive.

Special Techniques for Hanging Foils

Apply liner paper to create a smooth base for wallcovering over rough or uneven surfaces, such as paneled, textured or masonry walls.

Handle foils carefully. Do not crease or wrinkle the strips, and make sure to flatten out all bubbles immediately when hanging.

Use soft smoothing brush to avoid scratching or burnishing the reflective surface. Do not roll the seams: tap gently with smoothing brush to bond seams.

Special Techniques for Flocks & Fabrics

Use clear adhesive or traditional wheat paste, as directed by manufacturer. Clear adhesive will not bleed through and stain fabric surfaces. Some wallcoverings may direct you to apply adhesive to the walls instead of to the strips.

Use dry paint roller with soft nap, or a soft brush with natural bristles to smooth flocks and fabrics. Stiff smoothing brush bristles might damage the wallcovering surface.

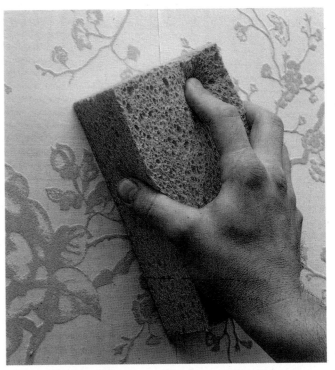

Tap seams with a smoothing brush or your fingers to bond the seams. Do not use a seam roller on flocks, fabrics or other specialty wallcoverings.

Keep adhesive off face of flocks and fabrics, if possible. Remove wet adhesive immediately by blotting with a slightly damp sponge.

Wallcovering Ceilings & Walls

Wallcovering a ceiling is easier if you have another person help you. Let your helper hold one end of the accordion-folded strips.

Dust your hands with talcum powder when handling dry wallcovering, to avoid smudges. When planning a ceiling job, remember that the pattern on the last wallcovering strip may be broken by the ceiling line. Since the least visible ceiling edge is usually on the entry wall, begin hanging ceiling strips at the far end of the room and work back toward the entryway.

If you plan to cover the walls as well as the ceiling, remember that the ceiling pattern can blend perfectly into only one wall. Plan the ceiling job so the strips will blend into your chosen "match" wall.

How to Wallcover a Ceiling

1 Measure width of wallcovering strip and subtract ½". Near corner, measure this distance away from wall at several points, and mark points on ceiling with pencil.

4 Cut out a small wedge of wallcovering in the corner so that strip will lie smooth. Press the wallcovering into the corner with a broadknife.

2 Using marks as guide, draw a guide line along length of ceiling with a pencil and straightedge. Cut and prepare first wallcovering strip (page 100).

3 Working in small sections, position strip against guide line. Overlap side wall by ½", and end wall by 2". Flatten strip with smoothing brush as you work. Trim each strip after it is smoothed.

5 If end walls will also be covered, trim ceiling overlap to ½". Leave ½" overlap on all walls that will be covered with matching wallcovering.

6 On walls that will not be covered, trim excess by holding broadknife against corner and cutting with sharp razor knife. Continue hanging strips, butting edges so that pattern matches.

1 Measure from corner a distance equal to the wallcovering width minus ½", and mark a point. Sketch out seam locations, and adjust if necessary (see Hanging Plan, pages 98-99).

2 Draw a plumb line at marked point, using a bubblestick. For wall that must match pattern of wallcovered ceiling, draw the plumb line straight down from first ceiling seam.

3 Cut and prepare first strip (page 100). First, unfold top portion of booked strip. Position strip against plumb line so that strip overlaps onto ceiling by about 2." Make sure there is a full pattern at ceiling line.

4 Snip top corner of strip so that wallcovering wraps around corner without wrinkles. Use open palms to slide strip into position, with edge butted against plumb line. Press strip flat with smoothing brush.

5 Unfold bottom of strip, and use flat palms to position strip against plumb line. Press strip flat with smoothing brush. Check carefully for bubbles.

6 Trim excess wallcovering with sharp razor knife. If ceiling is wallcovered, crease edge of wall strip with broadknife, then trim along crease with scissors to avoid punctures. Rinse adhesive off surfaces.

7 Hang additional strips, butting edges so that pattern matches. Let strips stand for about ½ hour, then use a seam roller to lightly roll the seam. On flocks or fabrics, tap the seams gently with smoothing brush.

8 With power turned off, hang wallcovering over outlets and switches. Make small diagonal cuts to expose the outlet. Trim wallcovering back to edges of opening with razor knife and broadknife.

How to Wallcover Around an Inside Corner

1 Cut and prepare a full strip (page 100). While strip cures, measure from edge of previous strip to the corner at top, middle and bottom of wall. Add ½" to longest of these measurements.

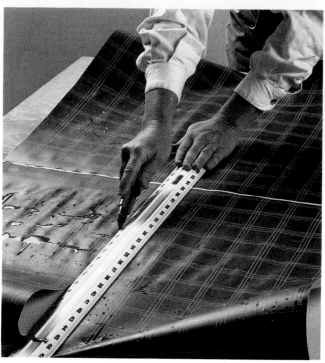

2 Align the edges of the booked strip. From the edge, measure at 2 points a distance equal to the measurement found in Step 1. Hold straightedge against the 2 marked points, and cut the wallcovering strip using a sharp razor knife.

3 Position strip on wall with pattern matching the previous strip, overlapping ceiling by about 2". Using open palms, carefully butt edges of strips. Strip will overlap slightly onto uncovered wall.

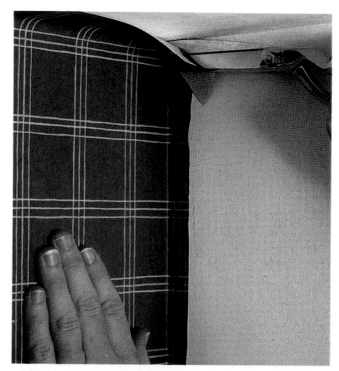

4 Make small corner slits at top and bottom of strip to wrap the overlap around the corner without wrinkles. Flatten strip with smoothing brush, then trim excess at ceiling and baseboard.

5 Measure width of the remaining strip. Mark this distance from corner onto uncovered wall and mark with pencil. Draw a plumb line from ceiling to floor on new wall, using a bubblestick.

6 Position strip on wall with cut edge toward corner and factory edge against new plumb line. Press the strip flat with a smoothing brush. Trim at ceiling and baseboard.

How to Wallcover Around an Outside Corner

7 If using vinyl wallcovering, peel back edge and apply vinyl-on-vinyl adhesive to lap seam. Press seam area flat. Let strips stand for ½ hour, then roll seams and rinse using a damp sponge.

Outside corners can usually be wrapped around without cutting the strip and drawing a new plumb line. If corner is not plumb, follow directions for inside corners, except add 1" to Step 1 measurement to allow for a wider wrap.

Wallcovering Around Windows & Doors

Do not try to precut wallcovering strips to fit the shape of windows or doors. Hang a full strip right over the casing, then smooth the strip before trimming the edges of the door or window. Make diagonal cuts to fit the wallcovering around sharp corners. To avoid damaging the wood on these diagonal cuts, use scissors instead of a razor knife.

If short strips are hung directly above and below opening, make sure these strips are hung exactly vertical to assure a good pattern fit with the next full strip. Do not trim the short strips until the last full strip has been hung. This allows for small adjustments in case of slight mismatches.

How to Wallcover Around Windows & Doors

1 Position strip on wall, directly over window casing. Butt the seam carefully against the edge of the previous strip.

2 Smooth the flat areas of wallcovering with a smoothing brush. Press strip tightly against casing.

3 Use scissors to cut diagonally from edge of strip to corner of casing. Make similar cut in bottom corner, if hanging around a window.

4 Use scissors to trim away excess wallcovering to about 1" around inside of frame. Smooth wallcovering and press out bubbles as you work.

5 Hold wallcovering against casing with broadknife, and trim excess with sharp razor knife. Trim overlaps at ceiling and baseboard. Rinse wallcovering and casings using a damp sponge.

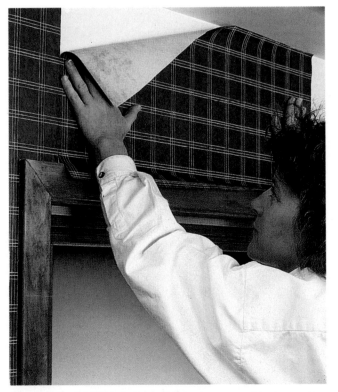

6 Cut short strips for sections above and below window. You may find scraps that will match the pattern and fit these spaces. Make sure small strips are hung exactly vertical to assure pattern match with the next full strip.

(continued next page)

7 Cut and prepare next full strip. Position it on wall with edge butting previous strip so that the pattern matches.

8 Snip top and bottom corners diagonally from edge to corners of casing. Trim away excess wallcovering to about 1" around inside of window or door frame.

9 Match seam on bottom half of strip. Trim excess wallcovering to about 1" with scissors. Flatten strip with smoothing brush.

10 Hold wallcovering against casing with broadknife, and cut excess with sharp razor knife. Trim overlaps at ceiling and baseboard. Rinse wallcovering and casings using a damp sponge.

How to Wallcover a Recessed Window

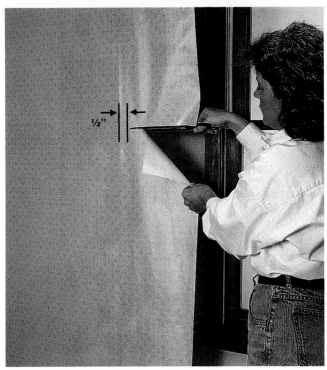

1 Hang wallcovering strips so they overlap recess. Smooth strips and trim excess at baseboard and ceiling. To wrap top and bottom of recess, make horizontal cut at the halfway point to within ½" of the wall.

2 From horizontal cut (Step 1), make vertical cuts to top and bottom of recess. Make small diagonal cuts to corners of recess.

3 Fold the upper and lower flaps of wallcovering onto the recessed surfaces. Smooth the strips and trim at the back edge. Wrap the vertical edge around the corner. Hang wallcovering around window, if needed (pages 112-113).

4 Measure, cut and prepare a matching piece of wallcovering to cover side of recess. Side piece should slightly overlap the top and bottom of recess, and the wrapped vertical edge. Use vinyl-on-vinyl adhesive to glue overlapped seams.

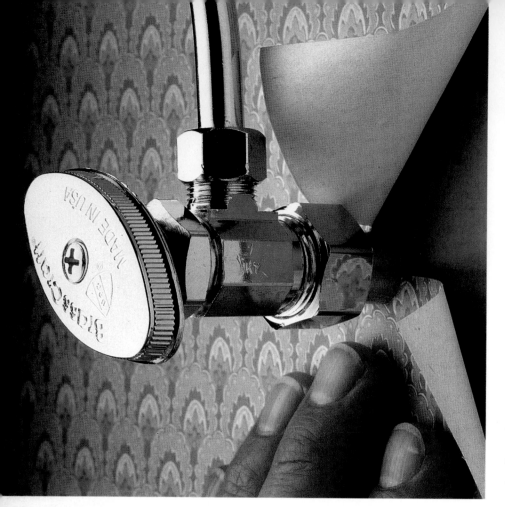

Wallcovering Around Pipes, Radiators & Fixtures

Hanging wallcovering around sinks, pipes and other obstacles requires cutting into wallcovering strips. Hold strip so that patterns match, and cut from the edge closest to the fixture. If possible, cut along a pattern line to hide the slit. At the end of the slit, cut an opening to fit around the fixture. On wall-mounted sinks, tuck small wallcovering overlaps behind the sink.

How to Wallcover Around a Pipe

Escutcheon

1 Pull out escutcheon from wall. Hold wallcovering strip against wall so that pattern matches previous strip. From closest edge of strip, cut slit to reach pipe.

2 Press strip flat up to pipe with a smoothing brush.

3 Cut a hole at the end of the slit to fit around pipe. Butt the edges of slit, and brush smooth.

How to Wallcover Around a Wall-mounted Sink

1 Brush wallcovering strip up to edge of sink. Cut horizontal slits in wallcovering, leaving ¼" overlap at top and bottom of sink.

2 Trim wallcovering around side of sink, leaving slight overlap.

3 Smooth wallcovering. Tuck excess wallcovering into crack between sink and wall, if possible, or trim overlap.

How to Wallcover Behind a Radiator

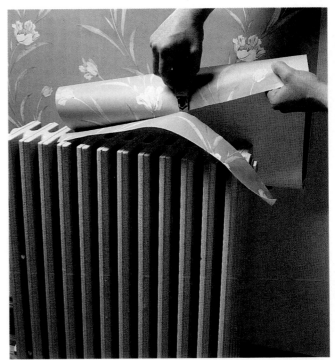

1 Unfold entire strip and position on wall. Smooth strip from ceiling to top of radiator. Use a flat wooden yardstick to lightly smooth the strip down behind the radiator. Crease the wallcovering along baseboard with the yardstick.

2 Pull bottom of strip up from behind radiator. Trim excess wallcovering along crease line. Smooth paper back down behind radiator with yardstick.

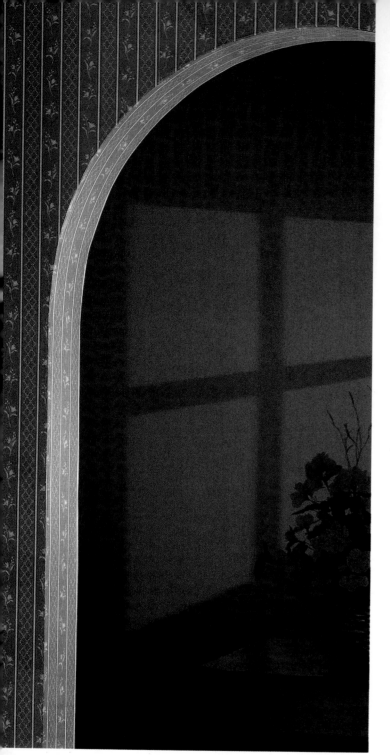

The left side is a large photo.

Wallcovering Inside an Archway

Cover the inside surface of an archway with wallcovering after the walls are finished. Wrap the wall strips around the corners of the archway, then hang a matching strip or wallcovering border around the inside surface to cover the wrapped edges. On curved archways, make a series of small slits in the wall strips so that the wallcovering lies smoothly. Use vinyl-on-vinyl adhesive to hang the archway strip.

How to Wallcover Inside an Archway

1 Some wallcoverings are available with matching borders that can be used to cover inside of archway. Or, measure inside of archway and cut archway strip from standard wallcovering. Strip should be ¼" narrower than inside surface of archway.

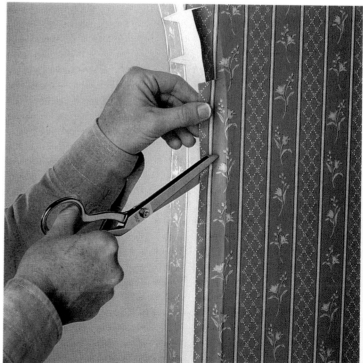

4 Make small slits in wallcovering along curved portion of archway, cutting as close as possible to wall edge.

118

2 Hang wallcovering on both sides of archway, with strips overlapping archway opening. Smooth the strips and trim excess at ceiling and baseboards.

3 Use scissors to trim overlapping wallcovering, leaving about 1" excess.

5 Wrap cut edges inside archway and press flat. If adjacent room is to be wallcovered, wrap wall-covering around edge of archway from both sides.

6 Coat back of archway strip with vinyl-on-vinyl adhesive. Position strip along inside of archway with ⅛" space on each edge of strip. Smooth strip with smoothing brush. Rinse strip using damp sponge.

Covering Switch & Outlet Coverplates

As a finishing touch, cover the switch and outlet coverplates with matching wallcovering. For plastic coverplates, use a vinyl-over-vinyl adhesive.

If you wallcover the coverplates in guest bathrooms and bedrooms, you may want to install switches with illuminated levers for the benefit of guests.

Tip: To fully blend switches and outlets with walls, paint receptacle face, switch levers and coverplate screw heads with matching paint.

An easy way to match outlets and switches is to purchase new clear plastic coverplates. Cut wallcovering to fit into the coverplates, and cut openings for switch levers and receptacle faces.

How to Cover Switch or Outlet Coverplates

1 Remove coverplate and reinsert screws. Cut scrap wallcovering that matches area around switch or outlet. Fasten patch over outlet or switch with drafting tape, so that pattern matches wall.

2 Rub surface of patch to emboss outline of outlet or switch screws. Remove patch and mark embossed reference points in pencil on the back side.

3 Lay the coverplate facedown over the wallcovering patch so that outline lines up with holes in coverplate. Mark the corners of the coverplate on the patch.

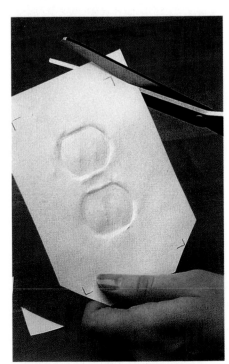

4 Trim scrap ½" wider than coverplate on all sides. Trim corners of patch, cutting just outside corner marks.

5 Apply vinyl-on-vinyl adhesive to coverplate and patch. Attach coverplate to wallcovering. Smooth out bubbles. Wrap overlap around back and tape edges in place.

6 Use razor knife to cut openings in coverplate. Tape the wall-covering pattern specifications on the back of the coverplate for future reference.

Hanging Wallcovering Borders

Wallcovering borders add an elegant accent to either painted or wallcovered walls. Hang a border as a crown molding around a ceiling, or as a frame around windows, doors or fireplaces.

Use a border along the top of wainscoting, or as an attractive chair rail on painted walls. You can even use a wallcovering border to frame a favorite art piece. Many wallcovering designs have complementary borders which are sold by the linear yard. Or you can create your own border by cutting narrow strips from full-size wallcovering.

How to Hang Borders

1 Plan starting point so that mismatch seam of border will fall in an inconspicuous area. For chair rail borders, use a level and draw light pencil line around room at desired height.

2 Cut and prepare the first strip. Begin at a corner, and overlap border onto adjacent wall by ¼". Have a helper hold the accordion-booked border while you apply and brush it.

3 For seams that fall in the middle of walls, overlap border strips so that patterns match. Double-cut seam by cutting through both layers with razor knife. Peel back border and remove cut ends. Press border flat.

4 To "cut-in" flush with wallcovering, overlap border onto wallcovering, then use straightedge and razor knife to cut through underlying wallcovering along border edge. Pull up border and remove cut wallcovering. Press border flat.

How to Miter Border Corners

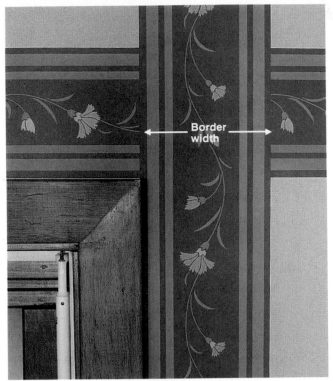

1 Apply horizontal border strips so that they run past the corners with overlap greater than border width. Apply vertical border strips along the side casings, overlapping top and bottom strips.

2 Check position of strip to make sure important pattern designs will remain intact at diagonal cuts. Remove and adjust strips, if necessary.

3 Holding straightedge at 45° angle from casing corner, double-cut both layers with razor knife. Peel back ends of border and remove the cut pieces.

4 Press the border back in place. Let border stand for ½ hour, then lightly roll the seams and rinse the border with damp sponge.

Finishing Touches

After you have finished wallcovering a room, check for final touch-ups while the job is still fresh. Pay special attention to the seams: if you rolled the seams too hard, or rolled them before the adhesive set, you may have squeezed too much adhesive from under the edges of the covering. These edges will look tight while they are wet but will bubble after the covering is dry. Reglue the edges of the seam as shown.

Standing close to the wall, look down its length, against the light. With a strong sidelight you see any bubbles or loose spots in the coverage.

How to Fix a Seam

Lift the edge of wallcovering and insert the tip of glue applicator under it. Squirt adhesive onto the wall and gently press the seam flat. Let repair stand for ½ hour, then smooth the seam lightly with a roller. Wipe seam lightly with damp sponge.

How to Fix a Bubble

1 Cut a slit through the bubble using a sharp razor knife. If there is a pattern in the wallcovering, cut along a line to hide the slit.

How to Patch Wallcovering

1 Fasten a scrap of matching wallcovering over the damaged portion with drafting tape, so that the patterns match.

2 Insert the tip of the glue applicator through the slit and apply adhesive sparingly to the wall under the wallcovering.

3 Press wallcovering gently to rebond it. Use a clean damp sponge to press the flap down and wipe away excess glue.

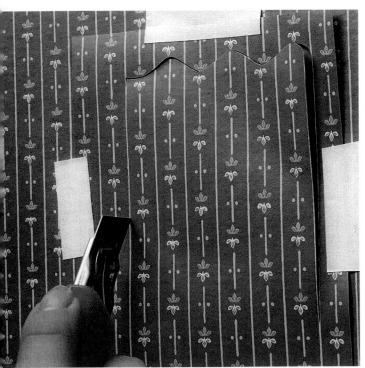

2 Holding razor knife blade at 90° angle to wall, cut through both layers of wallcovering. If wallcovering has strong pattern lines, cut along lines to hide seams. With less definite patterns, cut irregular lines.

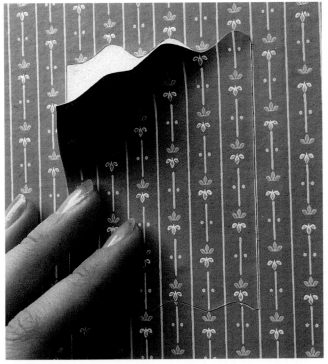

3 Remove the scrap and patch, then peel away the damaged wallcovering. Apply adhesive to the back of the patch and position it in the hole so that pattern matches. Rinse patch area with damp sponge.

Index

Cy DeCosse Incorporated offers a variety
of how-to books. For information write:
Cy DeCosse Subscriber Books
5900 Green Oak Drive
Minnetonka, MN 55343